FORENSIC ASTROLOGY FOR EVERYONE

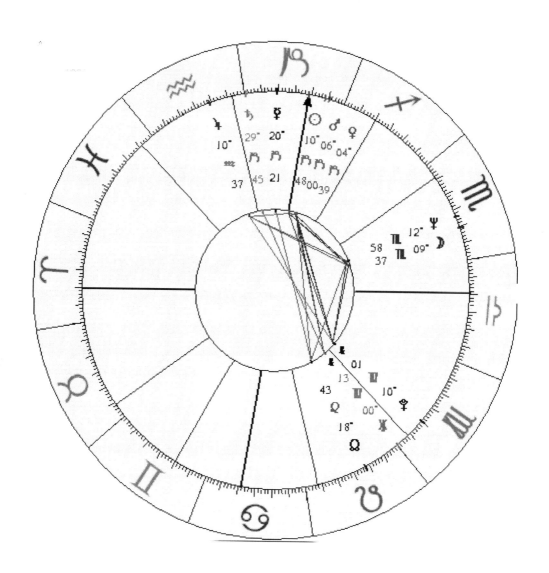

BY CAROLINE J LULEY

YOU DON'T NEED TO BE AN ASTROLOGER TO USE ASTROLOGY TO LOCATE LOST OBJECTS, FIND MISSING PERSONS, SOLVE MYSTERIES OR PREDICT THE OUTCOME OF EVENTS.

TABLE OF CONTENTS:

SECTION ONE: BUILDING A FOUNDATION FOR FORENSIC ANALYSIS

FORWARD:

This paperback is a compilation of two ebooks which I wrote previously in a planned series of 5 lesson guides. These books were designed to introduce and then teach, step by step, the art of analyzing forensic astrology charts for purposes of solving cold cases. The practice of Forensic Astrology as used today is part science and part art and requires an indepth knowledge of the basics of traditional astrology. In the first book, eBook One: An Introduction to Forensic Astrology, I showed the student how to build the foundation for forensic analysis. There is a bit more to it than drawing up other charts, although natal charts as well as composite and progressed charts can be quite a task in and of themselves. But you will have to use all that you know in those practices and then some in order to get to the meat of the forensic analysis, which can be, and should be, quite complex.

In the ebooks, as well as in this paperback, I deliver my teaching in such a way that even a beginner will be able to draw up forensic charts and analyze them. You do not have to be an astrologer to learn how to do this from my instructions. If you have never drawn up a chart and do not know much about astrology, then start with the first section of this book and work your way through the lessons until you are where you need to be. For those of you with a background in Astrology, even those of you who can work with charts already, you might want to move onto section two to begin with. But remember this is a whole new system, one that I devised, solely for the use in difficult investigations and there is a lot that is different from the system you are currently working with. There are elements of all methods I've ever used, including horary systems, as you might expect, but the overall system I use is a bit different. You may be able to use some of my methods and marry them to your own and end up with an even better system for this kind of work. The field is not new but it is not explored nearly enough. I think the time is right for forensic work in astrological analysis. I believe it has much to offer in a world where so many people are left with unanswered questions and the authorities who normally gather these answers are simply overwhelmed. At the very least, charts can offer insights and small clues that might otherwise be undiscovered.

I intend section one to work as a field guide. This should be the one that you always go to for reference, as a structure and foundation for all that comes after. If you are a beginner, this may be the only book you will need to learn how to work with astrology. There is much to astrology that you will not need to know in order to do this work so traditional tomes teach much more than you need to learn. Of course, if this system wets your curiousity and you find yourself wanting to move into other methods and systems of astrology, then there are tons of books out there that will help you move on to those places. But this should be your point of reference for all the work to come, most especially if you are a beginner.

PART ONE: A SUMMARY OF FORENSIC ASTROLOGY

The term "forensic" astrology is sort of misnomer but it is the closest description we can give this sort of work. The word "forensic" implies legalities, legal evidence to be used in court, in fact, and since astrology is not considered to be admissable in court as evidence, it cannot honestly be called "forensic". But it does, at that point of perfection, provide information to help an investigation move along and aid investigators in obtaining the kind of evidence that can be used in court. At the very least, these charts help investigators gain insight into cases that have simply stalled and gone cold. It holds out promise as a field of study that can be utilized in solving cases and is just as viable as psychic profiles or other intuitive clues that are currently used in some cases. The problem, I believe, is in the development of a system that can be used by just about anyone, including people who do not know astrology from mythology. I believe it can only be implemented by dedicated students of astrology who not only master all levels of the science but also have an ability to use the art of intuition. Although there are stringent rules with astrology, perimeters you really cannot stretch, definitions you cannot change and, in this regard, it is a science, there are also those gut feelings, instincts and even archetypal interpretations that can be used in doing this work. To this extent, astrology is both science and art.

PART TWO: MY BACKGROUND IN FORENSIC ASTROLOGY

I have worked with investigative methods for many years now. It all started when I joined the Astrological Research Guild in the 1980s and spent hours listening to their lectures on the results of their studies. One such study was an effort to find links in the charts of serial killers. To find a distinctive pattern in the charts that would allow us to isolate these people before they started killing. But the results were dismal. It turns out that although astrology is extremely diverse it is also very structured at the same time. There is no aspect or position that is found in one chart that is not found in many others, making many serial killers charts similar to the charts of ordinary people like you and me. Mars in Scorpio, for instance, may be seen as a sexual position but does it make a person a pervert? Mars in the fourth creates problems with the father but does that have to create an angry, violent child? Angry enough to end up killing people? No, it doesn't. In fact, many people have tough charts and they end up being saints and heroes. And many people have a bunch of trines and sextiles and end up bums and crooks. As in every area of life, the end result of all events depends upon the soul who experiences those events. Some people make lemonade out of lemons and others allow the lemons to sour their entire life.

So how on earth can astrology help in these cases, after all? Well, I did abandon their idea of isolating aspects or placements that would determine a murderer and moved on to other studies. In that process, I discovered a book, "Horary Astrology" by a brilliant woman named Geraldine Davis that subsequently changed my direction. I found it on the floor of an old bookstore with a 50 cent sticker on the worn red cover. I could not resist any book on astrology being sold for only 50 cents so I grabbed it. I realized at the time that it had been published in the 1930s and was probably long outdated by "new" discoveries but I love reading traditional writings on this science. To my pleasant surprise, the book took over my life. I just could not resist putting it to the test. I must be honest and admit that in no way did I come close to being as astute as this woman apparently was, but the results of my tests were amazing. I had done similar experiments years earlier, in the 1970s when I was still in my 20s, on the theories presented in Llewellyn George's tome, "The A to Z Horoscope Maker and Delineator", also a book written in the first part of the last century but proven to be invaluable to my work. In working with Llewellyn George's book I had done rectification of birth times and planetary seconds of arc using logarithms and was swept away by experiments that kept proving how well astrology worked over and over and over again. I mean, when you ask people when they got married, or when they got divorced or when their father died and then you turn it back, seconds of arc by seconds of arc and end up with the exact moment of their birth, accurate according to actual birth certificates, it's just a little convincing. So I was eager to try the same experiments with horary astrology.

For the next few years, and for every year of my life since, I have solved personal mysteries using her methods. For instance, I found a crystal ring that had fallen into the toe of a shoe that I hardly ever wore at the bottom of my closet. I found an empty envelope that once held a large sum of my money on the floor of a bathroom in the mall after I'd left the mall and discovered my loss miles away. I found a bag full of albums that I had left in a movie theatre and had been stolen by an employee. The albums were stashed in his locker. I discovered who had stolen the money from my purse on a night out with friends. I found a department store credit card that disappeared from my bedroom in the bedroom of one of my closest friends. Not all of these were happy events but they were conclusive. Horary astrology works. And I'm not making any of this up. I was so impressed with what I had learned that I just could not resist using it all the time.

At the same time in my life, some other radical changes occurred in my way of working with astrology. I went to apply at a psychic fair to be an astrologer for their group and this was a successful group that traveled all over the state in the 1980s. But I was rejected because I couldn't "do it in my head" and was running around with an armful of books. I never even thought of making that jump, from depending upon books to creating a personal system that would allow me to "do it in my head". I have since made that jump. Now, I can look up at the sky and, knowing what day of the month it is, tell you what sign is rising, where the Moon is and the aspect between the Sun and Moon, as well as what house the Moon and the Sun are both in. This all by simply knowing whether the Moon is waxing or waning and the day of the year. Of course, if you work with astrology as much as I do, you also know where the major planets are because planets like Saturn,

Pluto, Uranus and Neptune stay in the same place for years at a time. And then, from this, what the aspects are between these planets and the Sun and Moon and maybe also what house positions they all have at the same time. All from looking at the Moon and knowing the time of day.

My favorite part of astrology has always been the experiments and doing charts meant to find things and solve mysteries. This is what would eventually lead me to use it forensically. But the truth is, I did not get there quickly and not for a long long time. Not until the summer of 1990, when the Gainseville student murders took over my world. Those murders were so horrible, so gut wrenching, so consuming, that I would run home from work every day at 5 pm and watch the news, just to hear if they had solved these crimes. I don't think anybody on local TV talked about anything else until the spring of 1991 and even then they continued to speculate about spring break and kids in Gainseville for years to come. To make a long story short, I did the charts on these cases at the time and sent my findings to the Gainseville task force. I doubt they paid them any mind but it was first leap of faith. And what did those charts tell me? I have posted the charts and my findings on my blog, Forensic Astrology, where I profile many different cases and show you, both in advance and in retrospect, what forensic charts did, do or could have revealed at the time. And, hopefully, at the same time, demonstrate to you just how valuable and truthful these charts can be. You can visit the blog at http://forensicastrology.blogspot.com.

NOTE: HOW TO USE THIS BOOK

First of all, let me beg you not to run away from this after the first few sections. I have lost a lot of budding would be students over the years because they look at astrology and think they can't swallow something this big. And it is true that it's huge. There are so many things you can learn and then use with astrology that it boggles the mind and then withers the ambition. But I am not going to put you through all of that. I am not going to teach you astrology, force you to memorize it and then move you through a hundred other layers. It is going to be deep anyways, I can assure you that. It has been a lifetime study for me and most of it is second nature but I will try hard to keep it in mind that many of my readers don't know Mars from a Martini. LOL. I am going to shovel a lot of big spoonfuls of information into your mouth and make you swish it around. But I promise you that you do not have to swallow it all. In fact, you don't have to memorize anything in order to use my system. And you don't need to "know" astrology in the regular sense. Just hang in there.

This book should be kept as a sidekick to all the others you may use, as an eternal source of reference for all the work you will be doing. This book contains the basic principles of astrology as well as the basic techniques comprised in my method of forensic analysis. But nothing more than you will need to know to do what I do. You can use this book as a reference book no matter how far you dive into the study; it will be a good source point even for those skilled and talented astrologers who are intimately familiar with traditional analysis. My method is based on a great deal of tradition, from basic astrology to horary astrology to psychological astrology and so on. Although I am the first and perhaps the only one to do this the way I do, it is not, as a whole, that far away from the traditional forms. As a student and writer of astrology I specialized in ancient traditions like the arabic parts formulas and rectification, I also specialized in special configurations like domino stelliums and grand squares and also in the area of fixed stars and their definitions and applications. I wrote extensively on all of these subjects and learned quite a bit in the process. So, in many ways, my methods are based more on ancient and arcane studies than they are on current fads. But I am not going to make you learn all of this. You are going to use this book, and especially section one, as your guideline not only during the learning process but even after you've begun doing it on your own.

So I intend this book to introduce you to the basics of astrology while building a foundation for extensive work in forensics. This book should serve as the foundation and ongoing reference material you will need as you become proficient in forensic astrology. I am going to use sample charts and show you how what I say can be seen in the charts. I am going to give you exercises that you can do that will help you gain insight. And then I will have you practice on your own before giving you two quizzes (with the answers) that you can use to compound your skills. At the end of section one you should be drawing up forensic charts and starting to read them. So consider this book your eternal guide to reading forensic charts and while you are looking for lost objects, pets, missing persons and even trying to find dead bodies, you will have a simple resource that will do most of the work for you. You won't have to memorize a thing.. unless you want to.

PART FOUR: THE BASICS OF FORENSIC ASTROLOGY

Getting the Right Data

The very most important part of this work is in gathering the right data. This data, in all cases, should include the time (in hours and minutes), the location (including city, state or country as it applies) and date (including day and year). You must get a specific time so that you have starting point. You will quickly learn that you cannot do charts for every hour in a day or even for a twelve hour period because they lose clarity. An accurate time, preferably a specific hour of the day or night when the subject was last seen, last heard from or reported missing, is the best point from which you can begin your charting. A few hours window will be acceptable to those of you with some experience but not to those just starting out. It will take practice and depth of knowledge to allow you to work with a spread of many hours. In the gathering of this information, you have to be extremely careful because in the first few days of a murder or a missing persons case, information flies fast and free and is often not accurate. Always go to the law enforcement websites to obtain times, dates and locations. Do not allow family and friends to push hearsay or their own versions of the truth. The cops only present information that they have verified and verified and verified again. In many cases I have worked on, the family has a different take than the police. This can happen for all sorts of reasons, the most often being wishful thinking or disbelief of another's testimony. Never fall into these traps. Get your information from the most objective, professional source possible. And wait until the cops finalize this information and never go with preliminary information. Wait until it's repeated more than once. And double check any changes in information that appear on websites or newspapers. Misprints and misinformation are both rampant.

If you do discover that you did not have certain facts that you should have or that some of the facts you have are not accurate, redo the charts immediately and discard any previous charts you may have been working on. I have kept various charts around without thinking it mattered only to discover that I was continuing to work on an inaccurate chart. Times and locations are the data that change the most often, with people saying they heard from the victim at 4 am and then saying later it was midnight. They will also often say they saw someone at the store and then later say, no, it was at the school.. Or some other such nonsense. So be careful. If you can't get varifiable data then refuse to do the chart. If you are working directly with a private party on a case that does not involve the public or police and there is no information on the internet or in newspapers, then you will have to take the data from the source. In these types of cases there are hardly ever any discrepancies. But be sure to ask questions and to get clear answers you completely understand.

From another vantage point, you can get too much information and this can alter your ability to see the charts clearly. Again, without any criticism for grieving family and friends, you can often get an avalanche of emotional information that is not at all helpful and can, in fact, be detrimental to your work. You need to remain unattached, dispassionate and clear headed. This is often hard as you read the details of many cases, especially those involving young women and children, but you must work at it. Over time, you will get to the place where you work within the chart without any outside consideration at all. You may cry about it later but while you are at work, it has to be science first. I have upset my share of friends and family with my charts, where they just could not believe that their loved one or friend would have even been in the situation the charts describe. I have been tempted, believe me, to rewrite the whole darned thing just to stop the anger and pain. Still, it is about Astrology and I encourage them to dismiss it if that works for them but I cannot. I am an Astrologer, after all. And if you are to be an Astrologer, as well, you need to put the science first and let the emotional pain and anger take care of itself over time.

Creating the Event Chart

The first actual practice lesson you will work on is to create an actual event chart. Do not draw up a chart for just any data; you want to have an actual event chart to work with. Hopefully, after you draw one up you can use the same one throughout this book for all the exercises and experiments you will be doing. This way you can become intimately familiar with a particular chart and eventually be able to extend that familiarity to any event chart you work with later on.

In this day and age, you do not need to be a grizzled Astrologer to draw up a chart. Gone are the days of sitting at a desk with big books, drawing up dials from scratch. You don't have to rectify times and locations for sidereal time so you won't need a table of houses. You do, however, need to know the location of the event, including city, state or country. In some methods, you need to know the latitude and longitude of that location, as well. Not all astrology software have every location on the planet loaded into a database. You also do not have to move planets by minutes for every hour of a day in an ephemeris as we used to, which have planet positions and degrees for the first hour of the day and then for the next day and so on but not by the hours of a day. A lot of things can happen in a few minutes so you need to be tight with time, down to minutes and, in some cases, seconds. I have a method of rolling time forward and backward that I will teach you in this book. This method makes it easier to work with more flexible timeframes.

Anyways, my point is that it's much easier these days to create a chart, whether for a birth or other event, than it has been in the past. Reference books no longer need crowd Astrologers closets or bookcases. You can buy software, both for simple calculations and for more complicated tasks. You will only need the simpler software that can deliver a simple chart. For those of you who do not wish to buy software, for whatever reason, you can use the Astrolable online free charting system, which is what I use to create the charts I present on the blog. It is a Placidus system using the Tropical zodiac. In short, it's a western system and the one I habitually use in my own work. You can access this chart by going online to http://www.alabe.com/freechart/. You can also buy their fantastic charting softwares on the same site and many of them are inexpensive. I definitely recommend using one of the many softwares available for creating charts. It is far less time consuming and fantastically more accurate than doing it by hand. So even if you've never done a chart before in your entire life and are scared to death of it, this is easy. Just go to the free site first and draw up your first chart. After you get better at it and feel more comfortable about doing it, then you can consider buying software and books that will help you do even more with Astrology.

For our purposes here I want you to draw up your first event chart using data from a real case. This can be a solved or unsolved case, it doesn't matter except that a solved case can show you how the astrology comes out in the end. But also remember that solved cases are the hardest to get accurate information about because once a case is solved the media and the police stop making this information available to the public. The media likes to carry on about all the titillating details (consider the Bundy, Dahmer and Rolling cases as examples) but they don't go over the timelines after the case is solved. So this information often disappears from websites and newsletters. In these types of cases, if there is one you really want to tackle, it is likely you will have to buy a book if one has been written about the case in question. True crime books are often, but not always, detailed and careful about many specific facts, including timelines. But no matter how this turns out for you, it is a fact that you will be doing most of your charts for those cases that have the best timelines and details. There are many cases you will not be able to analyze, however much you wish you could. If you already have the timeline, date and location for a solved case you are familiar with, please feel encouraged to use this. But either solved or unsolved cases are useful. You make the choice that suits you.

Get the information about your chosen case from reliable sources. If you get the data from a website or newspaper, check with the local police or with police funded sources like Americas Most Wanted. Missing Persons groups that sponsor websites are usually reliable. Sites like http://www.missingkids.com and http://www.usamissing.com are great resources for data. If nothing gives this information to your satisfaction, then go to the FBI website (http://www.fbi.gov/wanted/kidnap) or to the local sheriff or police site for the area in which the crime occurred. State law enforcement agencies all have websites and contact information and you can even call them on the phone if you wish.

Once you have the data you need, go to http://www.alabe.com/freechart/. Use their form and fill in the data and then submit for the chart. When the chart is produced, right click on it and save it to your hard drive. Make a note of what directory you saved it to. Later on you will use a photo editing program to access the gif. This is the easiest, fastest way to produce a chart and now you have it in a place where you can email it, add it to a text file, paste it into a .pdf or post it on the web like I do on the blog. I am going to do an example chart for you to follow and compare with yours. I am going to use a well known unsolved case and display the dial below. I will use it as an example to show you what I'm talking about as I move along. You can use it to compare to your own chart and apply what I show you to your own chart, for your own interpretation.

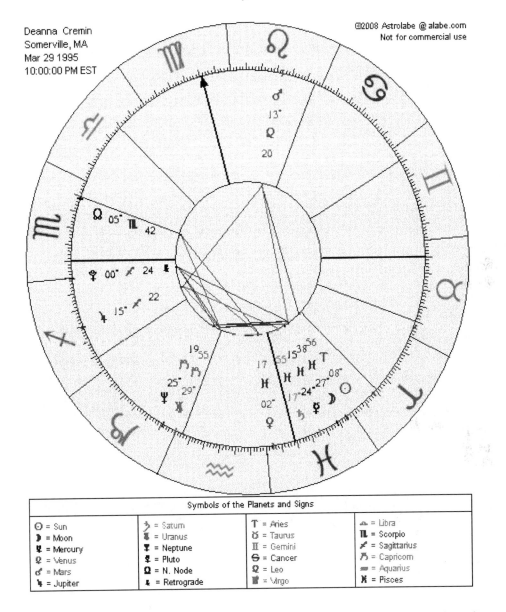

Deanna Cremin
Somerville, MA
Mar 29 1995
10:00:00 PM EST

©2008 Astrolabe @ alabe.com
Not for commercial use

Symbols of the Planets and Signs			
☉ = Sun	♄ = Saturn	♈ = Aries	♎ = Libra
☽ = Moon	♅ = Uranus	♉ = Taurus	♏ = Scorpio
☿ = Mercury	♆ = Neptune	♊ = Gemini	♐ = Sagittarius
♀ = Venus	♇ = Pluto	♋ = Cancer	♑ = Capricorn
♂ = Mars	☊ = N. Node	♌ = Leo	♒ = Aquarius
♃ = Jupiter	℞ = Retrograde	♍ = Virgo	♓ = Pisces

This chart is for the cold case murder of Deanna Cremin who has been missing since 1995. The chart above was drawn for the date she was last seen, March 29, 1995, in Summerville, Middlesex County, Massachusetts. This time for which the chart has been drawn is for the time she was expected to return home and was first known to be missing. Here are the details of the Cremin case from Wikipedia:

"On March 29, 1995, Deanna Cremin followed her usual Wednesday routine of going out with friends and visiting her boyfriend. She was supposed to be home by 10 pm; when she was not home by midnight, her mother, worried, tried unsuccessfully several times to reach her on a pager that the girl carried. Her boyfriend, considered to be the last person to see Cremin alive, admits walking her home that night, but says he left her halfway, as he often had during their year long courtship.

Cremin's body was found at 8 a.m. on March 30, behind a senior housing complex, less than a block from her home. She was found by two children she babysat for, taking a shortcut on their way to school. Her body was lying on its back, and mostly undressed. She had been strangled."

We have a basic overview of the case from authorities. We have known timelines as given to police by family and credible witnesses. Deanna was 17 at the time so she was on her own and not being overseen by adults. She had actually been with her boyfriend before being found the next day behind a senior housing complex. I was not sure, at first, what this referred to. Was this a old person's housing complex or was this senior dorms in a college? So I did a bit more digging to be sure I had the right information before I continued with the chart. I ended up on a website with a testimony by her mother (http://www.unsolvedmysteries.com/usm444678.html) which explained that this was actually both; there was a senior living complex for the elderly and an elementary school near where she was found. It was this information that let me know that the charts are viable. I will explain this in the next section. From that site:

"In Somerville MA March 30, 1995, on Jaques Street the body of my 17 year old daughter Deanna Cremin was found close to our home behind a building near the elementary school she once attended by two children who she once babysat. She had been strangled to death. The last person to have seen her alive was her boyfriend, Thomas L. who live nearby. It has been five and a half years and the investigation is still active." This is from her mother.

And from TruTV online forum:

"The lifeless body of 17-year old Deanne Cremin was discovered on the morning of March 30, 1995, behind an elderly housing project on 125 Jaques Street, Somerville, Massachusetts. She had been strangled and left hours before." You can see this entry at: http://boards.library.trutv.com/showthread.php?283371-Unsolved-murder-of-Deanna-Cremin-has-NEW-Information...Please-Help!.

You will find that you often have to locate many different sources on a case before you can say you have the facts. Do not be afraid to look at several sites and to ask questions of people who say they have the facts until you think you have the whole story. There is nothing more useless and heartbreaking than spending many hours on analyzing a forensic chart and thinking you have finally cracked it only to discover your facts were wrong and you have to start over.

To get your own copy of this chart to follow along while I analyze it, go to http://astrolabe.com/freechart and enter the following information: Name- Deanna Cremin; Time: 10:00 pm; Location: Somerville, Massachusetts. Click on submit. When the chart appears, right click on it to save it to your hard drive. Name it so you can find it later.

Determining Viability of a Chart

There are various methods that Astrologers use to determine the viability of a chart. One of the favorite methods is to check the degree on the rising sign or first house cusp. If this degree is less than 5 degrees or greater than 25 degrees, it is generally considered to be a useless chart. In my experience this is just not always the case. Sometimes the degree on the first house cusp directly relates to the birth chart of the victim or the perpetrator and since you most likely do not have access to a natal chart for both of these people, it is possible the chart is viable and you won't know it. So I have developed other methods of determining viability. My favorite method is to see if something in the chart correlates to the facts. For instance, if the reports from witnesses have the victim at the church just before she or he disappeared and the chart shows the presence of a church, a preacher or other religious reference, you can pretty much say that this chart is viable. This method is not cut and dry and it does require some involved knowledge of Astrology. If you do a few charts and learn as you do, you will get better at making this judgement. Also, if you are intuitive or are willing to work at developing your intuition, then this method will become easier with practice. Another method of determining the viability of a chart is to determine if the first house ruler describes your victim accurately. Let's say that the chart shows us Mercury in the fifth house and the victim is somebody's child. Mercury is the traditional ruler of all children. The presence of his type of Astrological pointer will prove the chart viable most of the time.

The first house ruler in our example chart is Mars. You know this because the sign Scorpio is rising on the left side of the dial as you face it from the computer. Scorpio is ruled by Mars. Notice that Mars in this chart is placed in the ninth house. You count houses from the first house around towards the right side of the dial and then up and back around to the left side or first house. The ninth house often shows areas that are outdoors, such as highways, parking lots, fields or meadows and such. It is almost always a marker for outdoor events and can often describe the woods. It has rulership over sporting activities as well so it often describes outdoors areas with woods where people hunt and fish. In this case we know that Deanna was found outside. This is clearly shown by the first house ruler placed in the ninth house. I have some more to mention as it relates to the ninth house and this chart. Her mother also said that her body was found close to a senior housing complex, a place for the elderly. Saturn is in the fourth house of this forensic chart. Saturn is the ruler of death, dieing and old age. In a chart where you are trying to locate the body Saturn often marks that body. In this chart, it is showing the body in the fourth house, which indicates it is close to a home or residence of some kind. Saturn is in Pisces which is the sign associated with old age and dieing. Saturn is very close to the cusp of the fourth house, the lowest point in the chart that is also called the "nadir". In forensic charts, this cusp is often read as the door to a home. She was found right outside these homes, just as if she was "at the doorstep"(the fourth house cusp) of an elderly home (Saturn in the fourth).

Pluto, the planet that most often describes chaos, change, violence, radical action and the underworld, is positioned here in the first house. Deanna, we know, died a violent death. Jupiter, the natural ruler of the ninth house, is also positioned in the first house, in the sign Sagittarius. Jupiter is in dignity because it is in it's own sign, Sagittarius, which it naturally rules. It is also powerful because it is in the first house. Any planet in the first house of any forensic chart takes on great power and influence. Jupiter is the ruler of sports and sporting events but also rules schools and education. In the facts above her mother said her body was discovered behind a building near an elementary school. All of these markers, in general and together, tell us very clearly that this chart is viable. Everything works in harmony. She was found right outside these homes, just as if she was "at the doorstep" (the fourth house cusp) of an elderly home (Saturn in the fourth), she was found outside (Mars in the ninth), she had been violently murdered (Pluto in the first) and the body was close to an elementary school (Jupiter in the first).

To summarize viability, it comes down to a few factors. Something in the event chart should dovetail closely with the known facts. Also the rising degree should not be at the last degree or first degree of the sign unless this works with the birth chart. The first house ruler or sign and planet that resides at the first house cusp should be descriptive of the victim and his or her known circumstances. Otherwise, if it just doesn't make sense, then it's not viable. If you can't read it, you can't analyze it, so let it go.

Here are some thumbnail guidelines for those of you who are new to Astrology:

1. The first house is located at the easternmost point in the chart, which is the left side of the dial when you face it. The first house ruler is the planet that rules the sign on that cusp. The rulers of each sign are:

Aries is ruled by Mars
Taurus is ruled by Venus
Gemini is ruled by Mercury
Cancer is ruled by the Moon
Leo is ruled by the Sun
Virgo is ruled by Mercury
Libra is ruled by Venus
Scorpio is ruled by Mars and Pluto
Sagittarius is ruled by Jupiter
Capricorn is ruled by Saturn
Aquarius is ruled by Uranus and Saturn
Pisces is ruled by Neptune and Jupiter

2. The first house ruler must be located in the chart. You can find houses by counting downwards from the first house, to the bottom of the chart, back up to the opposite side and then up to the top and back around to the first house. Locate the planet that rules the first house in one of these houses. Each of these houses rule the following:

1st House rules the person, their personality, appearance and behavior. It also tells you what they are doing and where they are. Planets in the first house can tell you if they are doing what they want to do or if they are being forced. Useful in determining the difference between a run away case and an abduction.

2nd House rules their belongings, the material things they have with them or they are concerned about. It often indicates banks, safe deposit boxes, purses, trunks of cars and storage units, among other things. When you see planets in this house they often tell you what the person is concerned with. Is the case about money? If so, you will see it here.

3rd House rules their movements. This most often indicates whether they are on foot or in a car. It can describe the vehicle they are in. It can describe the direction and/or general area they are travelling in. It also describes interactions, conversations and communications such as the use of phones. Cell phone pings can be tracked in charts by using the planet that rules this house and any planets placed in it.

4th House rules the home, residence or current location. This house will tell you if the subject is in a home or not. Often you can determine whose home this is and what it looks like from the planets and aspects involving the fourth house. It can also indicate the home of the subject and how far the subject may be from their family home. This house is shows the family in general.

5th House rules the outside interests of the subject. Entertainment, sports, music, pleasure, children, parties, alcohol and drug use, all of these are seen in this house. Depending upon what planets are in this house, you can tell if there are children involved, if there is a party going on, if this is a drug or alcohol case, if someone is playing games or sports. When a child goes missing from a baseball field, for instance, you are likely to see that event in this house.

6th House rules the work or employment of the subject. It can also indicate health or sickness. Sometimes this house shows you that the subject is very ill and in grave danger of death. This house can also point to people the subject works with or places where the subject works. If co workers are involved in the case, you will see them here. You will also see it if the subject is with a sick person who cannot help themselves. You will be able to see this after you have located the abductor in the chart, which I will show you how to do later in this book.

7th House is usually the abductor. It is also the murderer, kidnapper, accomplice or co conspirator in the forensic chart. If the subject were a runaway, for instance, and had help getting away, the ruler of this house will show you who that helper was. Most of the time, this house will show you the friend, the lover, the spouse, the stranger or the sick person who intervened and caused your subject to be missing or dead. It most often describes the murderer.

8th House rules the dark side of life. It often describes the death of your subject and is integral in the development of a "death pattern" in the chart. I will tell you about death patterns later. The eighth house also describes criminals, desperate people, drug addicts (especially combined with markers in the fifth house), sexual activity, other people's money and the theft of that money. It most often describes the death of your subject but also often describes a criminal or desperate person if there was one involved in the event.

9th House rules many different things in a chart, as I already pointed out in the previous section. It can rule the outdoors in general and outdoors activities like hunting or camping. It can describe schools, student, teachers and places of learning or teaching. It can refer to travel, to moving over long distances, such as on major highways, interstates or flying on planes. It can also refer to foreigners, people from other places or immigrants, both legal and otherwise. And the ninth house can also refer to legalities, laws, lawyers, authorities and police. You will have to really develop both your understanding of the planets and signs that appear in this house as well as your own intuition and insight to analyze this house properly in the forensic chart.

10th House rules the public. In general, in most forensic charts, it rules the public attitude towards a particular case and can mean media attention. Cases that have charts with strong planets or fixed stars in this house often become media sensations. But it can also indicate public spaces like government buildings, in one instance, or public spaces in general. It often reads that the subject was "out in the open", in the public, so to speak, in a place where they could be easily seen. This house is prominant in cases where victims are snatched right out in the open rather than taken from a bedroom at night, for instance. As you get better at this, you will be able to use this house to determine whether a case will ever be solved and how long that might take.

11th House rules friends, acquaintances and people recently met. If the subject has met somebody recently who now plays prominantly in the case, this person will appear in this house. Often you can see the subject among their friends or with a close friend here. Subjects that disappear from group gatherings can be traced with this house. Also use this house to locate lovers outside of the marriage or secret alliances no one knows about.

12th House rules the end of life and the loneliness of dieing. It can also describe hidden areas, dark places or small places of confinement. Think coffin. We are bound to our deaths by simply being alive so consider this house to show confinement or being held against the will. This house is integral in the development of the "death pattern", which I will explain to you later and can show where the body is buried. Planets like Saturn or Pluto in the twelfth indicate death, as can the first house ruler or the Moon in the twelfth.

Locating the Subject in the Chart

Before you can determine viability, you need to know how to locate the subject. Once you determine the viability of a chart and begin to analyze it, you will begin with the subject. The chart is all about the subject, after all, although it will have other players and ongoing events. To locate the subject, you must first analyze the first house. The first house is the cusp (spoke) on the wheel (dial) that sits on the absolute eastern horizon. In the sample chart you will see that this house is ruled by Scorpio. It also has two planets inside it, Pluto and Jupiter, both in the sign Sagittarius. You can determine the sign glyphs using the legend at the bottom of the dial. So, as an example, this chart shows Scorpio as the descriptor for the victim. Remember that this is only for the very first chart you create as you will create many more during the analysis. This chart is for the time that she was last seen or last expected and did not arrive. So this chart is the first chart we examine to determine what she is doing or where she is at that time. In this chart, at this time, she is described by the sign Scorpio, which is ruled by both Mars and Pluto.

So, the first house being Scorpio means that this chart has three rulers. Mars, the natural ruler of Scorpio and Aries, Pluto, the secondary ruler of Scorpio and the Moon, which is the natural co ruler of all event charts. So here we see that Mars is in Leo in the ninth house. This is your primary director describing the victim. Pluto is in Sagittarius in the first house, a secondary director. And the Moon is in Pisces in the fourth house, a natural director. So within the aspects and locations of these three planets we will be able to describe the subjects current location, activity and condition. We anlayzed these factors in the section about determining viability of the chart. But remember that forensic charts are fluid and will give information for everything that is sought for and can sometimes overlap. For instance, in this chart you will find information that correlates to her death but also to her condition prior to her death. You may see her actual death if this chart turns out to reflect her actual time of death. But even if it doesn't, it will give information related to her death. The positioning of certain planets and signs in houses related to death create what is known as a "death pattern" and this pattern often includes the ruler of the first house, the marker for the subject, as well as the Moon. Although I haven't gotten there, yet, I want you to know that the Moon is the co ruler of every single forensic chart, even those in which the Moon rules the first house.

I must say now, before we go any further with this, that analyzing Astrology charts is a fluid, living and evolving art that will depend greatly on your own insight and, in some cases, intuition. You will have to learn to read it as if it were a story unfolding in front of you, much in the same manner as psychics read tarot cards or palms. But this is not the same pyschic experience, although psychic abilities can be applied as well, because it is also a science which can be experimented with and demonstrated. Astrology can be just as hard and cold as physics or math. In fact, it uses both physics and math in it's creation and application. But you must learn to not only see it but to breathe it, to take it into yourself and make a part of your thought process in order to really own it. I know that sounds goofy but that is how I have come to use Astrology, to master it as you would a singing technique or a golf swing. You have to practice and give it a lot of thought; go out at night and look at the sky and see if you can tell the sign the Moon is in based on the time of year and whether it's waxing or waning. See if you can tell what sign is rising based on the time of day or night and where the Sun is. Once you can command it, you can master it. You don't have to be this good to do forensic astrology but it certainly helps you to succeed.

But even if you do not know Astrology, I can give you enough guidance to have you making up forensic charts and reading them. With practice, you will get better over time. If you are motivated by the idea of getting really great at this, you will buy books and study all the basics and get good at Astrology.

So now that we have located the victim in the chart, through the planets Mars, Pluto and the Moon, we how need to locate any other players in the case.

Locating Other Persons in the Chart

In most forensic charts, you have a subject who has gone missing, has been found dead, who is presumed dead; this person is assumed to have been abducted if they have not just run off. The next big step in determining which is the case is to locate the assailant. If the subject has been abducted, then there will be an abductor. If there is no abductor, or anyone else you can pin down in the chart, then it is possible they are a runaway. Sometimes you will locate another person but not see indicators that force was used and in that case you may have located a runaway with an accomplice or helper. Often it is the case that young women run off with lovers so this is a consideration as well. But the next order fo the day is to locate this second person in the chart, whether they are an abductor, a murderer, a friend, a lover or an accomplice.

In order to locate this other person you have to examine the seventh house. The seventh house is the cusp (spoke) on the wheel (dial) that sits on the absolute western horizon. It is exactly opposite the first house on the dial and represents enemies, attackers, lovers, partners, theives and murderers. In this chart, the sign Taurus rules the seventh house and this makes the planet Venus the marker for the other person, if there is one. Sometimes when you examine the seventh house you find a ruler (marker) that does not seem to have any purpose in the chart. I will show you later on how this can be. If this is the case, then you would say there was no abductor or kidnapper, that the subject was alone. But in most cases you will see other people and the seventh house is where you start.

In our example chart you can see that Taurus is on the seventh cusp with the planet Venus placed in the sign Pisces in the third house. Venus in Pisces is the person she is "next to meet" or next to arrive on the scene, so it will describe other people who influence events as they transpire. So in this case we will use Venus as the marker for her murderer. Remember we know she met with a murderer because she has already been found dead. Venus in Pisces in the third house indicates someone in a car, perhaps, because the third house rules vehicles. Although the third house can also describe a neighborhood or area where people walk around so this might be someone in her neighborhood. Gemini, the natural ruler of the third, indicates cities and places where people congregate and communicate so this would be in an area where other people frequent. Therefor, I would say that this person is on foot or in a car in a neighborhood near where Deanna was at this time and this would likely be in the city, a populated area, on a city street. Remember that the third house describes cars so even if the charts eventually prove that the assailant was not driving, he was likely on foot on streets where cars were present.

To see what the relationship might be between Deanna and this person, you check the aspects. In this case, I see the only aspect is a square between Pluto, Deanna's co ruler, and Venus. Pluto traditionally describes the underworld, mass changes, violence and use of force by individuals and by groups such as the police or street gangs. The square indicates that there was abrasion or difficulty; somebody resisted or tried to avoid something. Together, these two elements tell me that Deanna was grabbed by force, against her will, she fought and resisted but was assaulted and taken away. This aspect alone shows us that she was taken by force by someone and this was not consensual. The placement of Venus tells us that this happened on a street in a city neighborhood where other cars were traveling and people were not far away. It may have been near a phone booth (third house) or in an busy area of a city neighborhood. And if Deanna lived in an urban neighborhood, run through with small streets that are always busy with people and cars, then this may be where this happened. But the final analysis will only be created and considered finished after you have viewed all of the charts from every angle and combined all the various elements to a probable conclusion.

PART FIVE- BUILDING A FOUNDATION FOR ANALYSIS

Isolating House Cusp Rulers and Angular Planets

Before I keep leaping over fences and leaving you to figure out what I'm talking about, I want to address the house cusp rulers and angular planets. These are the only factors you will be considering in analyzing a forensic chart so you should be intimately familiar with them. The house cusp rulers are the signs that sit on each of the spokes of the wheel. In this chart, the first house ruler is Scorpio, the second house is ruled by Sagittarius, the third house by Aquarius, the fourth house by Pisces, the fifth house by Aries, the sixth house by Taurus, the seventh house by Taurus, the eighth house by Gemini, the ninth house Leo, the tenth house Virgo, the eleventh house Libra and the twelfth house Scorpio. In this chart, we have a phenomenon known as "interception" where some houses get intercepted inside of others, causing some signs to spread out over two cusps. This has great value in reading a forensic chart if the signs that cover two houses are covering angular cusps. I will explain.

What are angular cusps? These are the cusps at the four directions, east, south, west and north. These translate as the first, fourth, seventh and tenth houses. They are the primary areas of concern in a forensic chart, although the other houses can have importance as well if angular rulers are placed in them. None the less, you should always start with the angular cusps and their rulers before considering other cusps or placements in the reading. The first house cusp describes your subject; the fourth house cusp describes his or her location, most often a home and, if not, then a specific area; the seventh house cusp describes the murderer, the abductor, the lover or accomplice; the tenth house cusp describes the public view, the authorities and the nature of the events that transpire. Let me use our example chart as a guide.

We have already isolated the first and seventh house rulers, Mars, Pluto, the Moon and Venus. Now we are looking to see the location and nature of the area and events. The fourth house cusp is the southernmost spoke on the wheel, the one at the very bottom of the chart. In this case, it is ruled by Pisces and therefor marked by the planet Neptune. You will notice in the chart that some of the signs cover two houses such as the first house and the twelfth house both with the sign Scorpio on the cusp. This is the effect of a phenomenon called "interception". Due to the latitude for which an individual horoscope may be cast as well as inequality in the shape of the Earth, it sometimes appears that a sign is "intercepted" between the cusps of two houses while not being on either of them and another sign, usually opposite the intercepted sign, spreads out across two cusps. This is what has happened in our sample chart, shown above, and results in having Scorpio on the twelfth and first house cusps and the sign Taurus, opposite Scorpio, on the seventh and sixth house cusps as well.

At the same time you will notice that the signs Cancer and Capricorn are positioned in between two cusps but are on neither. The sign Cancer has been "intercepted" into the eighth house and Capricorn has been "intercepted" into the second house. This takes a lot of power away from the rulers of these signs. The planet Saturn, which rules Capricorn, would be considered to have no power in the chart except that here you find it placed at the nadir, or fourth house cusp, which is an angular house and thereby receives power. The Moon, which is the natural co ruler of the chart, would be considered powerless by Cancer's interception but in retains power as a secondary marker no matter what. The Moon, as well, is placed in the fourth house, which is angular and gives it even more power through placement. In many charts, this will not be the case. The intercepted signs and their rulers will have no power at all and will not be a part of the analysis.

In the next section I will explain the meaning of angular houses and cusps. Any planet placed in an angular house, which in every chart is the first, fourth, seventh and tenth houses and cusps, gains extra power through placement. The planet does not have to be on the cusp, it can simply be in the house, but in many charts planets both rule the cusps and are also placed in an angular house. This makes them doubly powerful. Only planets with power should be considered in a reading, regardless of your feelings about traditional rules. The only exceptions to this rule are the Moon, which is always a co ruler of the chart no matter where it is placed and Saturn, which if it is determined that the subject is dead, rules the bones and the body no matter where it's placed. In fact, you will use Saturn in most instances to help locate the remains. But every other planet in the analysis will have to be angular to be considered a part of the puzzle. In our example, Scorpio and thereby Pluto and Mars rule the first house and give information about the subject. Taurus and thereby the planet Venus rule the seventh house and give us information about other persons in the company of our subject. Pisces and thereby the planet Neptune rule the fourth house and tell us about the home, the location, the scenario where the actions in the chart are played out. And Virgo, thereby Mercury, rule the tenth house and tell us about the public situation, the involvement of authorities or powerful figures, whether or not the subject is in a public place when certain events occur and whether the case will gain attention from the public.

Analyzing Angular Houses

The houses of main importance are the angular houses, which are the first, fourth, seventh and tenth houses. Any planet ruling these houses or positioned in these houses has preeminent importance in the event chart. There are other houses that have importance at various stages of the analysis, but I will address them later. Let me give you an example. In the forensic chart that we are analyzing, you will see that the first house contains the sign Scorpio with that sign also on the first house cusp. This sign and house will tell us what we need to know about our subject at this particular point in time.

Consider that the first house cusp is positioned at exactly 26 degrees of the sign Scorpio with the remaining 4 degrees of the sign in the first house and the first 23 degees in the twelfth. You should examine the chart to determine if any other planets in the chart aspect that particular position (26 degrees of Scorpio). In looking at our sample chart, I see that Neptune is in 25 degrees of Capricorn. Capricorn is 60 degrees from the sign Scorpio and 25 degrees is only 1 degree away from 26 degrees so this is a very close sextile. Please check my reference table for the aspects and what they mean. Here I will give you a general summary.

Sextiles are weak aspects in the forensic chart unless they involve house rulers or planets placed in angular houses. In this chart, the first house cusp is 26 degrees of Scorpio and Neptune, placed in the second house in 25 degrees of Capricorn is a sextile aspect. The sextile is a common aspect and none of the planets in question are in angular houses (the first, fourth, seventh or tenth) so this aspect is unimportant and we will dismiss it. But here's what you will want to notice. The Moon, the natural chart co ruler (the Moon is the co ruler in every single forensic chart, no matter what) is in the fourth house, which is *angular*. The Moon is, as well, in the sign Pisces. This is a powerful position for the Moon, being that she rules the fourth house in the traditional chart. The Moon is in 27 degrees of Pisces and is 121 degrees away from the first house cusp. This makes the Moon *trine* to the first house cusp. The only factor that draws back on the power of this aspect is that the Moon is one degree beyond the Ascendant cusp and is, therefor, dexter, or separating from the aspect. This means that the effect of this aspect is waning away at the time for this chart, which is the time at which Deanna was expected home and she did not arrive. The trine is usually read as a postive aspect, a factor that makes things "easy" to come to pass and often facilitates certain situations, causing them to transpire. This aspect, at this point in the analysis, tells us one thing. She was in good spirits and is just beginning to "move away" from a *positive experience*. We know she was visiting her boyfriend and that she was going home from there at this hour or, at least, was supposed to be. From this aspect alone, we can reasonably assume that things went well with the boyfriend and that Deanna was happy or in good spirits when she "moved" from that location.

Even with this small amount of analysis it is easy to make assumptions. From my experience, it is best to leave assumptions out of the final analysis. Until you see all the contributing factors in the chart and have completed a full analysis, it is best not to jump to conclusions. The best chart analysis give the facts and leave it at that; no one is interested in your opinions, remember that. I have read many a chart where astrology told me one thing and I personally thought it must be wrong but in this work, the charts are to be trusted and my emotions are not. This should be your credo.

Never jump to conclusions, go with "your gut", react to your own emotions or change your analysis because it bothers you; always stick with the facts. For this type of work, forensic astrology, to be accurate and useful we must treat it as a science. So go about the work as if it were a science and seek out facts, no matter who strange they seem to you. The charts are ALWAYS right, in my experience, and my "gut" hardly ever is. So if you want to treat this as a serious study which is meant to produce serious results, then go about it in that fashion. So in this matter as we discussed above, we have a single trine creating a positive influence at the moment and the tendency is to say that Deanna was happy when she left her boyfriends so the boyfriend can't be guilty. First of all, it is not our job to determine innocence or guilt, we have to leave that up to the court system and a jury of peers. We are not judge or jury. Second of all, assumptions are a big mistake in this work; believe me, I have made a few that I had to eat later on. And they did not taste good. So train yourself to face every chart with a clear and open mind and do not assume anything unless the charts clearly show it to you. Anything else isn't science and it will ultimately be of no use... or, worse, end up embarrassing you.

REFERENCE GUIDE: How to Determine Aspects in a Chart

CONJUNCTION: This is when two planets are in the exact same sign and degree. Such as Neptune and Uranus both in 10 degrees of Leo. This is the aspect that creates the "new Moon" that you see every month. There are "spreads" for aspects used in various astrological systems and in the forensic chart there is a spread in the aspects as well. For most planets a spread of 8 degrees is considered acceptable for a conjunction. So if Neptune is in 10 degrees of Leo and Uranus were in 18 degrees of Leo, we would still call this a conjunction. This is a strong aspect.

SEXTILE: This is when any two planets are separated by 60 degrees. As an example, the Moon in the third house in 12 degrees of the sign Cancer is 60 degrees from any planet placed in 12 degrees of the sign Virgo. Each sign contains 30 degrees so you can count this way around the dial. If there is a planet in the forensic chart at 12 degrees of Virgo then these planets are sextile. A spread of 5 degrees is acceptable for a sextile. This is a weak aspect.

TRINE: This is when any two planets are separated by 120 degrees. As an example, the Moon in the third house in 12 degreesof the sign Cancer is 120 degrees from any planet placed in 12 degrees of Scorpio. A spread of 10 degrees is acceptable for a trine. This is a powerful aspect that can be a part of a larger, even more powerful aspect, called a Grand Trine. The Grand Trine has huge implications in a forensic chart but I will not go into that now. Do not worry I will come back to it later.

The Natural Zodiac

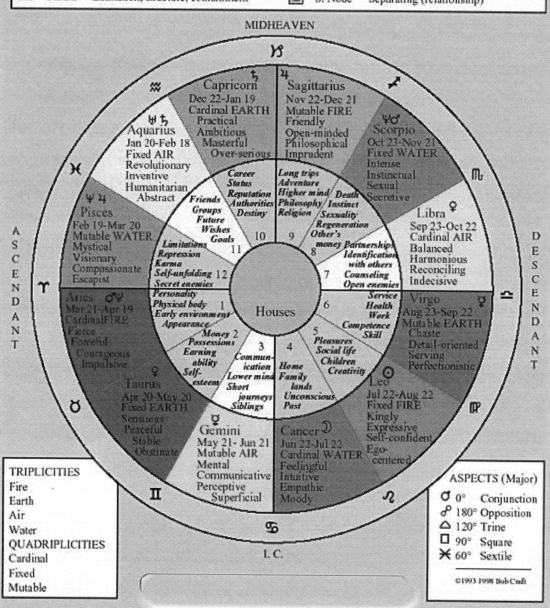

PLANETS

☉	Sun	Self-expression, will, assertion
☽	Moon	Response, intuition, feeling
☿	Mercury	Communication, thought, movement
♀	Venus	Harmony, love, beauty
♂	Mars	Energy, impulse, aggression
♃	Jupiter	Expansion, achievement, excess
♄	Saturn	Limitation, structure, containment

♅	Uranus	Change, liberation, rebellion
♆	Neptune	Nebulousness, illusion, imagination
♇	Pluto	Renewal, deepening, transformation
⚷	Chiron	Wounding, healing, re-integration
☊	N. Node	Joining (relationship)
☋	S. Node	Separating (relationship)

MIDHEAVEN

ASCENDANT

DESCENDANT

I. C.

TRIPLICITIES
Fire
Earth
Air
Water
QUADRIPLICITIES
Cardinal
Fixed
Mutable

ASPECTS (Major)

☌	0°	Conjunction
☍	180°	Opposition
△	120°	Trine
□	90°	Square
✶	60°	Sextile

©1993 1998 Bob Craft

SQUARE: This is when any two planets are separated by 90 degrees. As an example, the Moon in the third house in 12 degrees of the sign Cancer is 90 degrees from any planet placed in 12 degrees of Libra. A spread of 8 degrees is acceptable for a square. This is a powerful aspect that can be part of a larger, even powerful aspect, a Grand Square. It can also be a part of a combination aspect involving an opposition that is called the T Square. Both the Grand Square and the T Square have huge implications in a forensic chart but, again, I will save all of that for later.

OPPOSITION: This is when any two planets are separated by 180 degrees, making them effectively "opposite" each other. It is an opposition that creates the full Moon you see every month. A spread of 10 degrees is acceptable for an opposition. This is a powerful aspect that has huge implications in the forensic chart. This aspect can also make up part of the previously mentioned, T Square, which I will come back to later in the series.

INCONJUNCTION: This is when any two planets are 150 degrees from each other. This aspect is important in forensic charts and will be addressed later in the series. A spread of 6 degrees is acceptable for an inconjunction. This is a weak aspect.

Quality of an Aspect

You should always consider the nature of the aspect in question, whether it is a "strong" or a "weak" one which is determined by many factors, one of which is whether or not the aspect is applying or separating. If you've read my blog you've heard me reference aspects as "sinister" or "dexter". This is just shop talk for "applying" or "separating". This is very important in determining the overall strength of the aspect in question. So if the aspect is applying, this is a stronger aspect than an aspect that is separating. How do you determine if an aspect is applying or separating? Well, first of all you have to know the "order" of the planets in their motions. The Moon is the fastest planet and Pluto is the slowest. Therefor, if the Moon is in 5 degrees of Leo and Pluto is in 9 degrees of Leo, we say that the Moon is "applying" to a conjunction with Pluto (or as you have read on my blog, this is "sinister"). But if the Moon is in 15 degrees of Leo while Pluto is in 9 degrees of Leo, then aspect is "separating". Do not beat yourself up too much at this point on these details. I will come back to them over and over again in many different instances during the course of this study. So don't force down everything right now, swallow what you can comfortable ingest and leave it there. I will take you back here again later.

There are many other aspects that are peculiar to the forensic chart that I have not included here. I want you to be familiar with the traditional aspects first. I will address other aspects used in forensic analysis at a future point in the teaching so as not to confuse you on your path to understanding this system. However, I want you to take note at this time that an aspect is considered as strong or weak in accordance to it's direction, whether is is waxing or waning, sinister or dexter. Remember that all applying, waxing and sinister aspects are stronger and much more influencial than those that are separating or dexter.

NOTE: *What is an applying or separating aspect?* An applying aspect is where the faster moving planet is in a lower degree of the sign and the slower moving planet is in the higher degree. For example, the Moon in 12 degrees of Aquarius is APPLYING to a trine with the Sun in 18 degrees of Gemini. An applying aspect is also called sinister or waxing. It is a poweful aspect. A separating aspect is when the slower planet is in a lower degree of the sign and the faster moving planet is in a higher degree. For example, Mars is in 15 degrees of Leo and Jupiter is in 10 degrees of Aquarius, this is Mars in separation from an opposition to Jupiter. This aspect is weaker and less powerful. A separating aspect is also called dexter or waning.

The Meaning of Planets in the Forensic Chart

The meanings of the planets in a forensic chart are similar to the meanings of these planets in a traditional chart. But in the forensic chart, they are written in stone pretty much and are not subject to the variables that they may be in the birth chart. For instance, Mercury rules the mind in the birth chart so we can say a person is intellectual, stupid, brilliant, slow thinking, indecisive, etc.. in character and nature. This type of character analysis does not exist in forensic charts. Mercury in the forensic chart will have a specific, material definition that may have variables but does not change and does not take on other characteristics. You'll see what I mean when you read the list I am giving you for the general, unchanging descriptors for each planet in an event or forensic chart.

NOTE: No planet has any importance whatsoever in a forensic chart unless it is one of the following:

1. Positioned in the first, fourth, seventh or tenth houses (angular)
2. Ruler of the first, fourth, seventh or tenth houses (angular ruler)
3. Disposes of a planet positioned in or ruling the cusp of the first, fourth, seventh or tenth house
4. Is conjunct or opposite to any planet positioned or ruling the first, fourth, seventh or tenth house

If the planet does not have one of these positions in the chart, it is to be discarded and left out of the analysis of the chart in question. Remember to always combine the nature of the planet in question with the nature of the house it rules or is positioned in before determining exactly what the planet might represent.

The Planets:

The Sun

The Sun is usually a male influence but not always. You should doublecheck other aspects in the chart to find support for this idea. No planet gives a particular sex, even if that planet is associated with gender in the traditional chart. For instance, Venus and the Moon are not always women. However, when you find the Sun ruling an angular house and supported by other "male" planets like Mars or Saturn, you can pretty much assume that the Sun is presenting a male influence in the chart.

The Sun can be a place of great danger in the forensic chart. You should always check to see if any angular planets or chart rulers are placed within 17 degrees of the Suns' body. If so, then the person associated with this planet should be considered to be in grave danger and in danger of life and limb. This is especially true of the Moon in the forensic chart or any planet that rules or resides in the first house. If the Sun is placed in the first house along with other planets and these planets rule other angles, then it can be assumed that the subject is in grave danger from the presence of a male aggressor. Double this influence is Mars aspects as well.

The Sun in our sample chart has no real importance. It is not in an angular house and it does not rule an angular house. It's only influence will be how it interacts with the planets that do rule and reside in the angles.

The Moon

The Moon is always the chart co ruler, no matter what sign it's in or what house it's placed in. This makes the Moon an important marker in any chart, regardless of whether it is angular or not. So this makes any planet that aspects the Moon, disposes of the Moon or is in the same house with the Moon, aspected or not, to be important markers in the forensic chart. So you should read the Moon with the same importance as you do the first house ruler and consider any aspects to the Moon to be descriptors for your subject and their current condition or situation. The Moon is the only planet in the chart that does not have to be angular to be powerful and important in the analysis. In almost every case, the Moon is the secondary marker for the subject in question. Whether this subject is a missing person, a lost shoe or a runaway dog, the subject is the focus of the chart. The Moon is always the co ruler of the subject and equal in power to the first house ruler.

The Moon in our sample chart is in the sign Pisces in the fourth house. It is within 17 degees of the Sun's body, which is a special configuration (see below) that describes danger. The fourth house describes the home, residence, a place where people live and can simply describe the place where the subject is at the time. This combination shows us that our subject is in a residence or, at the very least, a building, where she is in grave danger. So this must be kept in mind during your analysis.

Mercury

In most forensic charts, Mercury rules children. If the subject is a missing or murdered child there are often questions as to what house to read for the ruler. This goes back to the ancient tradition in horary that the chart must be drawn for those asking about the missing person and not for the person themselves. And since most missing people are not adults and are frequently small children, the person asking is often the parent. So in these cases, the child is read in relation to the fifth house, which is the natural house for children. So in horary charts, the fifth house ruler is commonly read to describe the child. But I have found that many situations in today's world do not work with this practice. Often the person inquiring of the child is not the parent but a neighbor, a searcher, a concerned citizen or an astrologer. Also, today's children are often on their own at ages far younger than they had been in the past. I have found many cases of "latch key" kids on their own at 8 years old and even younger. Six year old children off on a bike with friends is also considered to be "on their own" because the decisions they make are their own and not dictated by an adult. In these cases, you just cannot read the fifth house ruler for the child. So how on earth do you make this work?

In any case where you are unsure and the subject is considered to a "child", or of an age where they should be supervised but are not, or if the person asking about the child is a stranger and not a family member, then go to Mercury and use it as the ruler. As in all cases, the Moon co rules in the cases of children, as well, so you would use the Moon and Mercury as the markers. This is the catch all, solve all, you should resort to if other placements are not working. Now, there are cases where the child was in a parent's supervision when they disappeared, this happens a lot, also. Mom is at the mall with her daughter and she turns her back long enough for the girl to disappear. Or mom is a POI. She was the last one to see the baby and the baby is dead. In all of these cases, where a parent played a role, then you must use the fifth house ruler for the child and the first house for the parent in question. This allows you to track the parent's actions, as well, and also determine if what they are telling you matches the charts. Often the case might be that the mother says the child walked away and the charts show the mother strangling her child. So use the first house for the parent and the fifth house for the child. You may also, in these cases, use Mercury for the child as a co ruler and the Moon as a co ruler for the parent, especially if it's mom.

And then there are the cases that don't involve children. How do you use Mercury in these cases? Well, there are many different ways that Mercury can work in a chart if you consider the nature of the planet. The most common I have found to be a vehicle such as a car or truck or a movement, such as walking, driving or running. If Mercury disposes of the first house ruler then it might mean this person is "on the move". Mercury naturally rules the third house where it describes cars, transportation, commerce and trade among "brothers" or, more often, "neighbors". So Mercury can indicate the business district, most definitely if it appears in the tenth house. A commercial district. And other planets with Mercury in that house might help you to figure out what kind of businesses are in that district. If Mercury is angular and rules the fourth house, then it is describing that house. Mercury rules "removeable" housing or housing that "moves". This might mean that the house is a trailer, a manufactured home, a campsite, an RV or any type of shelter than can be picked up or torn down and moved.

And what if Mercury rules the seventh house? Well, this can mean a few things in a forensic chart. The accomplice, murderer, abductor, enabler or partner in the matter may be a child. The thief may be a child. Of course, if Mercury rules the seventh and is placed in a different house, then a quick assessment of this house is necessary. Mercury rules the seventh from the tenth, this may well be a young person who is a "parent" himself, someone who has children at a young age. Or Mercury rules the seventh from the ninth, then perhaps this is a transient who comes from another country or, at the least, a different state. Or, let's say, that Mercury rules the tenth house and it's placed in the seventh. This would mean that the person in question may be a boss, a superior, a person who has authority or rank over the subject. This could be the father, it could be a police officer, it could be a prominent politician. It's up to you and what you know about the subject and their circumstances to make the best call as far as Mercury is concerned. For more reference on this matter, see the chart "Combining Planets and Houses in the Event Chart" presented below.

In our sample chart, Mercury rules the midheaven. This makes it an angular planet and it has some influence in this chart. Mercury is in the sign Pisces, which puts it in fall (no dignity) and it is placed in the fourth house. Mercury is a weak planet in the sign Pisces. Ruling the tenth from the fourth indicates that young people or children are playing a part in this event. Children are at the mercy of adults so this would explain the weakness of the placement. So wherever our subject is, there are children present. The tenth house is also the fourth from the seventh so we can assume that her abductor either lived with these chiildren or had them in his home for some reason.

Venus and Mars

Venus and Mars are extremely variable in the forensic chart. As angular rulers, they often describe people but you cannot just determine the sex from either planet. They often describe situations or actions. Mars can describe aggression. Mars in the first house can show aggression towards the subject, especially if Mars is disposed by an angular ruler or rules one of the other angles. If Mars rules the seventh and is placed in the first, it is a sure sign of violence towards the subject from another person. Mars in the tenth might describe a masculine presence but it can also describe a situation around masculine symbols such as auto repair shops or race tracks or other traditional male environments. Mars in the fourth house can show a male presence in the home. Mars ruling the seventh placed anywhere in the chart shows someone being aggressive in that area, the most important placements being the angular houses, of course. If Mars rules the seventh and is placed in the ninth, consider that this person may be a hunter or may be actually hunting something. The only variance here is the rulership of Mars over the first house. This is a marker for your subject and does not imply aggression. The house rulership of Mars will tell you who you are dealing with while the house placement of Mars will show you what that person is doing.

Venus is very soft in forensic charts. Most often, it depicts a mother or motherly presence. It does at times represent females but not always. I have seen it describe feminine males, males who are single parents, men who are artists, musicians, poets, etc.. Venus as a descriptor usually describes emotions between two people and is obviously a marker for romantic attraction. It will show you the romantic interest of the subject even if that person is a male. Sun and Venus together in a chart describes a couple, especially if those planets rule angles. But Venus is most often a soft player in forensic charts and is most often used as a descriptor rather than an active force.

In our sample chart, Venus rules the descendant. This gives it great power in the chart because it is the marker of our abductor. Venus is inside the third in the sign Pisces. This is a high octave for Venus, giving it even more power. This man is in his "baliwick" so to speak; he is in a safe place where he has control over everyone and everything. The third house indicates a moveable structure, a trailer, something that can be moved but also lived in. The sign Pisces is a water sign so this could be a boat. Pisces is a dual sign so this could be a second home for him; a place he goes to for privacy while his real home is elsewhere. This is possible. Keep this in mind while you are working up your analysis. In this chart, Venus is a very important planet. I will discuss more on this later.

Mars is in the sign Leo in the ninth house. It rules the first house and because of this also has great power in the sample chart. Mars is in the ninth house, in the sign Leo. This tells us where our subject is in better detail than the Moon, which has thus far told us she is in some place where people are living. We have also seen aspects that indicate it could be a boat.

Now, looking at Mars in the ninth, it is probably something rustic or outdoorsy. Again this could be a trailer, an RV, a boat, any residence that can be moved or traveled in. This relates to the placement of the seventh house ruler in the third. Mars in the sign Leo tells us also that this is a sunny place outside and that the residence, whether it be a boat or a trailer, is rather sunbleached and weather beaten. That is very possible with this placement. I will go into this even more later in this book.

Jupiter

Jupiter is very rarely a person. It can describe a person if someone comes along and this would be a descriptor for someone overweight, perhaps, and possibly on the "outside" of the situation. It can mean an onlooker was a witness. In some instances, it describes the police, especially if Sagittarius is on the ninth or tenth house cusp. But most often Jupiter describes scenery and objects. It can be a church, a school, a bakery, a candy shop, all sorts of things associated with traditional Jupiter. I have seen it in charts where the subject passed by a church or was found dead on school grounds. It is most often a place or scenery in the event, which can be determined by the sign and house where Jupiter is placed. As person, Jupiter may describe a priest, a teacher, a guru, a supporter, a chef or cook, a book publisher, etc... Always go to traditional astrology for support for your analysis.

In our sample chart, Jupiter is in the first house. This makes it a powerful influence in the chart, as well. Although it does not rule an angular house it does have power in it's placement in the first. Double that power because it is in it's own sign, Sagittarius. This tells us that there is something good on the side of our subject; she is either very educated, deeply religious, easy going and philosophical, etc... some quality to her nature and personality that gives her an edge. Luck is on her side. This placement alone would make me think that she might still be alive. More supporting aspects will have to be discovered in order for this prediction to be firmly made but Jupiter in the first is a good start.

Saturn

Saturn is the human body and in the traditional charts rules the bones. In the forensic chart, after the death pattern has appeared, Saturn describes the location of the body. Whereever it is in the chart, this will reflect where the body is at that point in time. Saturn in the second, the trunk of a car (the second is the twelfth from the third), Saturn in the third, the body is in the car but not in the trunk, Saturn in the ninth, the body is outdoors, most likely in the woods. Saturn in the fourth, the body is in a place of business. This can sometimes mean a warehouse or garage, especially if Saturn is in Gemini or Saturn is near Mercury. Saturn in the twelfth house means the body is very well hidden; if Saturn is in a water sign, look for other signs the body is in the water; if Saturn is in earth signs, it is probably buried; if Saturn is in air signs, it is on a high place, ie, a mountainside, a shelf in a closet, on a roof, papered into a ceiling, etc.. If Saturn is in fire signs look closely at the chart for further proof that the body was burned.

We do not have a death pattern in this chart yet so we do not see Saturn as being her body. This will only be necessary if we run charts for a later hour and find the death pattern there. So, at this point in our analysis of the event chart, we do see that Saturn is at the nadir. This is a powerful placement. It is also within conjunction with Mercury and the Moon, with both of these planets angular rulers. But looking to see that Saturn does not rule any cusps and is intercepted in the third, it does lose power. And, at this point in time, I will say that it has no more meaning than to assert that our victim will be staying where she is for quite some time to come.

Uranus

Uranus describes unusual, unexpected events and people. It also describes eccentricities, antiques, scientific equipment, laboratories, experiments, airplanes, airstrips, radios, radio towers, tv sets, tv stations, satellites, missiles. Unusual people; people who live on the edge; homeless people, brillant people. Combined with Neptune, a guru. Uranus may occassionally describe an upsetting event but most of the time, it describes locations. It is most often used to locate the body. If it is angular and has aspects to the rulers, especially Saturn, then it helps to describe the location. Always look for something unusual in the landscape and use the guides for Uranus in traditional astrology.

In our sample chart, Uranus has no power.

Neptune

Neptune in the forensic chart describes hidden factors, lies, pretensions and shams. It can also be a descriptor for plots and schemes, especially when combined with the node. In the fifth house it can describe drugs or alcohol. In the twelfth house, unconsciousness. In the eighth house, drug overdose. In the seventh house, a person who is not what he seems or a person no one knows about. Neptune often appears in the seventh house when one person is suspected of a crime but another second party, unknown and unsuspected, was involved. Neptune in the second, a scam for money. Neptune in the tenth, somebody lieing about their career or job. Neptune in the sixth, hidden illness.

In the sample chart, Neptune rules the nadir. Neptune is also placed in the second house in Capricorn. This is a further descriptor for the place where both the subject and her abductor are at the present moment. Neptune indicates someplace hidden, in shadow, a place no one knows about. The abductor has lied about this place in the past and no one knows where it is or that it even exists. That's the best guess I have for this placement in the chart at this time.

Pluto

Pluto usually describes chaos, destruction, upsets, fights, explosions, aggression, physical violence, disorder and riots. In the fifth or eighth house, can describe violent rape. In the eighth or twelfth house, violent death. In the fourth house, disruption in the current location, especially if it's a home or a place where people live. In the tenth house, disruption in a public place, a retail store, a business. In the sixth house, disruption or violence in the work place. Can also describe big changes at work that the subject finds unpleasant. In the third house, a car accident, especially if the third house ruler is in the ninth or the third house ruler is Gemini. Pluto ruling the fourth and placed in the fifth, the child was abducted.

Pluto is one of the most powerful planets in our sample chart. It is positioned at the Ascendant in it's own sign, Scorpio. Is is actually rising and will cross the Ascendant into the twelfth within minutes. Since Pluto describes chaos, upsets, rebellions, disorder, change and upheaval, let's say that the subject is suffering most of these effects at this time. She may very well be fighting for her life. Pluto would indicate at the very least that she was making every effect to strike back.

The Moons Node

The Moons Node is located in most ephemeris and will come in any chart you run online. There is both a south and north node of the Moon and they always oppose each other. By locating the north node, you will automatically know the placement for the south node. In most forensic charts, the node describes either events that conspire through either destiny or just by chance to create certain circumstances. You will see this often in charts where people are murdered. It is a metaphysical question of whether our death is destined or not. Many people believe that our death is preordained, even by murder. Other people believe that murder is a sin against God. Whatever you beleive, the node describes circumstances that bring things together. It is kismet. But the node has another meaning in the forensic chart and that is one of predetermination through plotting or planning.

The way it works in the chart will be determined by your analysis of the placements. The node can indicate that the murder was by design, that someone planned and thought about the act and then carried it out. In this manner, the death was predetermined and not a random, opportunistic event. This design is most often seen in charts of women who were murdered by stalkers. If you read the node carefully you will see who planned it and why. You will also see how long he had been stalking her. But I will come back to the node again in the series until I cover every angle but this enough for you for right now. Simply consider the node to be a marker for either a planned event where the murder was not at random or it was kismet, the coming together, through unexpected circumstances, two people, one of whom would murder the other. It will be up to you to determine which one applies.

In the sample chart we can see that the Moon's node is in the twelfth house. It is in the sign Scorpio, which also rules the first house cusp. It is disposed of by Pluto, which is in the first house near the Ascendant. This looks like a plot or a scheme directed at our subject, doesn't it? It is way too personal of a placement to be otherwise.

Fixed Stars

There are thousands of fixed stars in the heavens. Almost every star in every constellation is fixed and has a position in the chart. But only a few of those are truly useful in the forensic chart. Fixed Stars are often looked at in natal, transiting, progressed and even composite charts. The most common fixed stars that are considered are Alphard, Pleides, Spica and Cepheus. But there are hundreds more, not all of which really matter much. In the charts I read on the blog I often refer to certain fixed stars because of the traditional readings indicate they are negative or evil and such things are to be considered when people are murdered or abducted. In particular, Caput Algol is the most evil and violent of all and the Pleiades are the saddest. I have seen many charts in which the Pleides were right at the midheaven at the time of a vicious murder that ended up being infamous. A prime example is the Gainseville murders where 5 students were viciously murdered on 3 consecutive nights. In each event, the time advanced just enough to put the Pleides in an angular house. The hour at which each murder occurred literally advanced just enough to cause the fixed stars to be placed in the same manner each time. It was literally amazing when I saw it. It is another example of how Astrology teaches those who read it in unexpected ways.

Here are the fixed stars I use in the forensic charts and their actual placements. Also noted is their expected "effect" in the chart.

Schedir: 7 degrees 47 minutes Taurus: can indicate escape or being set free.
Pollux: 21 degrees 50 minutes Cancer: can indicate misfortune or calamity.
The Pleiades: (includes 7 stars: Alcyone, Asterope, Celaeno, Electra, Maia, Merope and Taygeta) 28 degrees of Taurus; can portend the death of many people, all at once or over time. A situation creating great sadness; tears.
Manubrium: 13 degrees 36 minutes Capricorn: can describe burning of a body or an arson.
Markab: 22 degrees 6 minutes Pisces; can describe shooting or being shot with a gun.
Kelb Alrai: 7 degrees 50 minutes Sagittarius; can indicate poisoning.
Polis: 28 degrees 13 minutes Scorpio: can indicate drunkeness or drug abuse.
Mirach: 29 degrees 01 minutes Aries: can mean drunkeness or drugs.
Unukalhai: 20 degrees 40 minutes Scorpio: can mean drugs.
Fomalhaut: 2 degrees 27 minutes Pisces: can mean drug addiction.
Betelgeuse: 27 degrees 21 minutes Gemini: can point to accidental death.
Vindemiatrix: 8 degrees 33 minutes Libra: can mean accidental death.
Dschubba: 10 degrees 10 minutes Sagittarius: can mean murder.

Alfard: 25 degrees 53 minutes Leo: can mean death by asphyxiation or strangulation.
Asellus Austral: 7 degrees 19 minutes Leo: can mean murder by decapitation or hanging.
Asellus Boreali: 6 degrees 9 minutes Leo: can mean murder by shooting.
Alfard: 25 degrees 53 minutes Leo: can mean death by drowning.
Scheat: 27 degrees 59 minutes Pisces: can mean death by drowning.
Caput Algol or Algol: 24 degrees 46 minutes Taurus: can mean murder, mayhem & bloodshed
Spica: 22 degrees 27 minutes Libra: can mean insight, kindness and a turn for the better
Vindematrix: 8 degrees 33 minutes Libra: can mean someone will be rescued.
Miram: 27 degrees 19 minutes Taurus: can mean someone is lying.
Al Hecka: 23 degrees 23 minutes Gemini: can point to pedaphilia or other deviation.
Hoedus: 17 degrees 14 minutes Gemini: can define lust, rape, lascivious behavior.
Bellatrix: 19 degrees 33 minutes Gemini: can describe obsessive lust and rape.
Sinistra: 28 degrees 21 minutes Sagittarius: can mean obsessive, wanton lust and sexual attack.
Asellus Austral: 7 degrees 19 minutes Leo: can describe a sleazy, criminal person.
Sabik: 16 degrees 34 minutes Sagittarius: can mean perversion or perversity.
Geidi Prima: 18 degrees 51 minutes Cancer: can mean rape has been committed.
Phecda: 29 degrees 4 minutes Leo: can mean a pathological sex addict.
Sirius: 12 degrees 42 minutes Cancer: can mean danger in the night.
Ras Algethi: 14 degrees 45 minutes Sagittarius: can mean a devious plot is involved.

With each of these stars the same orb of influence applies as with planets and cusps. Consider transits to the natal positions of these stars as well as their placement in the forensic chart. Practice placing them in the chart and seeing what they say. I use these stars as a last ditch effort in many charts were nothing is making sense. However, they can be used at any time and can lend a new dimension to a tired or confusing chart

In our sample chart, the following fixed stars have some prominence.

Markab, at 22 degrees six minutes of Pisces, sits between Mercury and Saturn in the fifth house. Mercury rules the tenth house. The Moon, nearby in 27 degrees of Pisces is close enough to be in conjunction. Markab describes a shooting or someone being shot with a gun. Remember this during your analysis of this case.

Fomalhaut, at 2 degrees 27 minutes of Pisces is nearly exactly conjoined Venus and both planets are just inside the third house and close to the nadir. In fact, this is a conjunction to the fourth house cusp. Fomalhaut describes drugs, people using drugs and drug addiction.

Scheat, at 27 degrees 59 minutes of Pisces is nearly exactly conjoined the Moon in the fourth house. Scheat describes death by drowning.

Sabik, at 16 degrees 34 minutes of Sagittarius is conjoined Jupiter in the first house. Sabik describes perversity; a perverted person.

Ras Algethi, at 14 degrees 45 minutes of Sagittarius, is conjoined Jupiter as well in the first house. Ras Algethi describes a devious plot or scheme.

So you must consider each of these placements in your analysis of the forensic chart and consider which ones appear to dovetail with the other placements. Always use the closest placement and the sinister placement, rather than a wide one that is waning. And notice which planets they are affecting. For instance, in the sample chart the fixed stars that aspect the Moon, the first house ruler and the nadir are much more important than the others that are aspecting planets that are in angular houses but do not rule any house of importance. For example, in this chart, the conjunction of Scheat to the Moon and Markab conjoined Mercury, which is the first house ruler, are the most important aspects of them all and should get first consideration.

Special Configurations

There are many special configurations in charts and many of them are used in traditional astrology. There are also many that are not used in regular charts but are used in horary and forensic work. You should be familiar with every single special configuration, what its meaning is and how it is working in your current chart. Many of these configurations can be firm assurance that what you are seeing has actually occurred. So every chart should be examined for these configurations and the meanings of each should be applied.

Reference Guide: Special Configurations & Assigned Meanings

Grand Trine:

A grand trine is a complete trine of all signs in an element. Such as you have three different planets in different water signs, all within a few degrees of a trine or exactly trine, and this is a Grand Trine. Mercury in 10 degrees of Pisces, Venus in 12 degrees of Cancer and Pluto in 8 degrees of Scorpio is a Grand Trine in water signs.

The Grand Trine faciliates events and makes things happen more easily, more readily. Where there might be obstacles in the path to action, the Grand Trine clears those obstacles easily. In the case of a murder or abduction, this trine shows us how the path to success was made easier for the killer or abductor.

There is a grand trine formation in the sample chart. It involves the trining of Mars in Leo to Sun in Aries to Jupiter in Sagittarius. Both Jupiter and the Sun are in exaltation and have great power already. Both the Sun and Jupiter are angular by placement. This makes the grand trine a tremendous faciliator in events that transpire in this chart. Aspects to each individual planet in the chart during the course of this event will give clues as to what really happened and why. And since grand trines are facilitating and cause things to happen, we have to look for instigators in the configuration. We find that the first house ruler, Mars, is a part of the configuration. This is a clear indicator that actions on the part of the subject helped to bring about the event in question. It will be up to the reader to analyze and figure out what actions the subject took that created this circumstance. And always remember this does not have to be a mindless, sinister or criminal action; if the chart contains inconjunctions the grand trine can often mean that the subject made a fatal mistake that allowed the abduction to occur and did so innocently.

Grand Square:

A Grand Square is a complete square between all signs of the same quality. Such as you have four planets in different cardinal signs, all within a few degrees of a square or exactly square, and this is a Grand Square. Mercury in 10 degrees of Aries, Mars in 13 degrees of Libra, Moon in 8 degrees of Cancer and Saturn in 11 degrees of Capricorn is a Grand Square in Cardinal signs. As the natural rulers of the angular houses, these signs have great power in any chart. If a planet or any planets in the Grand Square rule an angular house or are placed in angular houses, then the Grand Square has tremendous power in the forensic chart.

A Grand Square creates obstacles, challenges and impediments. It will be up to you, as the Astrologer, to determine how this applies; whether is the victim or their abductor who faces those challenges. In a forensic chart, this can lengthen the time frame for the victims longevity in the matter and can sometimes save their lives. If the Grand Square is powerful enough and it affects the abductor directly then you should consider that the victim will survive. However, if the Grand Square is powerful and affects the subject directly, then you are looking at a situation that the victim will never escape. Again, it will be up to you as the Astrologer to determine who and how the Grand Square is affecting the outcome of the event.

There is no Grand Square in our sample chart.

T Square:

This is a far more common configuration than either the Grand Trine or the Grand Square. The T Square is a partial square involving signs of the same quality. Mercury in 10 degrees of Aries, Venus in 12 degrees of Libra and Mars in 9 degrees of Cancer is a T Square. It will always involve an opposition of two planets that each square a third planet. The third planet is the short leg of the T and is the outlet for the energies created by the opposition. In our example, Mars creates the outlet for these energies. Consider if any of these planets rule an angle, are placed in an angular house or rule either the subject or the kidnapper. The nature of that planet will determine the outcome of the event. For instance, the first house ruler is opposed to the seventh house ruler and they are both square to Mars. Mars is the outlet of energies that have been generated by these two people. Mars is a violent aggressor in these cases and you may assume that the outcome of the energies, which may be agitated by circumstances, will be violence, most likely towards the victim, but not always. Again, it will be up to you as the Astrologer to determine who, why and how the T Square is operating in the event chart you are analyzing.

There is no T Square in our sample chart.

Bucket Formation:

A bucket formation is similar to a Stellium (below). It is a cluster of planets along one side of the chart with a few planets opposing them, making the chart look like a bucket with a handle. The planet or planets opposing the cluster do not have to be in opposing signs, merely being in an opposing house will do. This formation indicates a gathering of energies or sympathies in one area (or bucket) of the chart with outside forces putting pressure from the other side (or handle of the bucket). For instance, a group of planets in the fourth house create a small bucket while opposing planets in the tenth house create the handle.

There are no buckets in our sample chart.

Stellium:

This is a group of planets all together in the same sign or house. Planets in the same sign do not have to occupy the same house to qualify as a stellium and planets in the same house do not have to be in the same sign. In fact, many stelliums include planets in two or more signs scattered between two or more houses. This type of formation creates a great deal of energy in a certain area of the chart.

We have a stellium in the sample chart. Notice how there are four planets in the same house and four planets in the sign Pisces? Altogether these are 5 planets creating a bundle or stellium. One planet, the Sun, is in a different sign and one planet, Venus, is in a different house but these planets are all bundled together to create a stellium. This puts a great deal of energy and focus on the fourth house and the sign Pisces. This must be investigated further in the chart.

In this chart, the stellium includes the chart ruler, the Moon, and is therefor even more powerful. The seventh house ruler, Venus in Pisces, is the last sign in the grouping. This makes any aspects to this group more influencial in the chart and any special configurations that involve this stellium are also important. Jupiter in the first house in Sagittarius is in powerful dignity because it is in it's own sign and in the angular first house. Notice that Jupiter also trines the Sun and then squares a few planets in the stellium during it's transit. This makes Jupiter a powerful influence over the outcome of events in this case. Notice also that Jupiter trines the first house ruler, Mars, as well as the Sun, making it a part of a grand trine formation. The combination of the stellium and the grand trine in this chart creates an energy that cannot be ignored. Not only did the subject create a door of opportunity through actions that were taken but outside influences also converged on the situation and created interactions from others that could not be avoided. Any aspects to the stellium throughout the analysis will give a picture of what these outside influences were.

Domino Stellium:

This is simply a stellium in tight formation with all planets in the same sign within a few degrees of each other. They can be scattered throughout two or more houses but they must be in the same sign. This creates a domino effect when other transiting planets aspect each planet in the stellium, one at a time. There is a small domino stellium inside the greater stellium in this chart with Saturn, Mercury and the Moon within 10 degrees of one another in the sign Pisces. During the analysis you will have to pay special attention to any aspects made to each of these planets in turn. Since such fast moving aspects are usually made by the Moon and the Moon is a part of this stellium it is unlikely that any singular planet will translate light between them. However, planets that occupy angular houses that aspect any part of the stellium will have an effect on occurrences at that time and place.

Under the Suns Beams

This is a simple placement. It is any planet that is positioned within 17 degrees of the Sun's body. This is what is called being under the beams. So, for instance, the Moon is 17 degrees from the Sun, then you would say it was under the beams. Also, if Saturn were within 3 degrees of the Sun, you'd say the same. It is very unusual for more than one planet to be under the beams in a single chart. Although it always describes danger to life and limb, it is the most powerful when it involves the ruling or angular planet in the chart. When the Moon or the sign ruling the first house is within 17 degrees of the Sun's body you should read it as grave danger.

There are no planets under the Sun's beams in the sample chart.

Translating Light

This is the action of a faster moving planet aspecting two slower moving planets in swift moving time frame. The Moon is the swiftest moving planet in the chart so it is most often the translator of light. However, the translation can involve other fast moving planets like Mercury, the Sun, Venus and Mars under the right conditions. In the sample chart, for instance, we have the Moon in late Pisces moving towards Aries. Within a few hours, the Moon will enter Aries and first conjoin the Sun. As it does so, it will then trine Mars next. This would be a translation of the Moons light from the Sun to Mars. Although this aspect is not to happen for many hours in this chart, it will still occur and if it does occur while your subject is still alive and the event is ongoing, then it will have a powerful influence over the course of events. This aspect alone, when present, will cause things to happen. Watch it closely to determine what those things are.

Combust

This is a similar formation to being under the Sun's beams but it is a tighter configuration. I have rarely seen in it the charts I've done, even those where people were brutally murdered so this is a rare aspect. It would be any planet within 8 degrees ahead or behind of the Sun and in the same sign and house at the time. Any deviation of this pattern would be under the beams, of course, but it would not be combust.

In astrology, planets aspect each other down from the Moon, which means that only the Moon, Venus and Mercury can aspect the Sun. However, a planet can be combust without aspecting the Sun, as in the case of Uranus within 5 degrees of the Sun's body. This would make Uranus combust. This makes Uranus a negative answer in any question in the analysis. It usually neuters the planet in question and makes it weaker. This is no way a position of danger in the event. For the most part, it indicates a black hole or weak spot in the chart.

Via Combust Way

This is when any angular planet in the forensic chart is between 15 degrees of Libra and 15 degrees of Scorpio. There are violent fixed stars placed in this portion of the zodiac and any angular planet passing over these stars is affected by it. The only variation is when a planet is conjunct the fixed star Spica at 22 degrees of Libra, which gives not only relief from the influence but greatly enhances the positive. When a planet is along combust way it means the situation is very dangerous and critical. Someone is in real danger. You can tell who this someone is by noting which angle the planet rules. And remember, only angular planets matter. And if the planet is in the 22nd degree of Libra, there is a saving grace. We will go over this placement many times over before I am done with this series so don't worry if it feels confusing right now.

The only placement in the sample chart that is along combust way is the node. This would mean that any plot or scheme that arises in this event will be a dangerous one. But no individual is directly influenced by these fixed stars.

Collection of Light

This is where several faster moving planets aspect a slower moving planet. This creates an energy infusion into the house and the placement of the slower moving planet. In the sample chart, Pluto in Sagittarius at the Ascendant is collecting light. You can see that the Moon, Mercury and Venus are all sinister to a trine with Pluto. They are currently in the late degrees of Pisces but they are within the orb of influence and will soon be exactly trine to Pluto. They have all just passed a square aspect with Pluto and will soon be in Aries, where they will trine Pluto in Sagittarius. This collection of light by a planet in the first house doubles the effect and we can see here that Pluto has enormous influence over the events that are about to transpire.

Mutual Reception

This is a common aspect in forensic charts and is not as powerful as some of the others but it can never be ignored. This is where two planets are in each others ruling signs. For instance, Neptune rules the sign Pisces and Uranus rules Aquarius. If, for instance, Neptune is in Aquarius and Uranus is in Pisces, you have an example of two planets in mutual reception. I used these placements as an example because this has been a common aspect for the past decade. I find it in forensic charts all the time. This aspect alone will not cause things to happen but it can bring things to perfection. If the two planets are angular planets or the Moon, then this means that whatever is indicated by the planets in question is doubled in influence and can be considered to be true.

In our sample chart we have Mars in Leo and Sun in Aries. These planets are in mutual reception. Since Mars rules the Ascendant, the mutual reception brings the Sun into the forefront of the chart and as events transpire you will have to take the Sun into consideration as a player in this chart where it would otherwise not be.

Peregrine

In traditional Astrology this placement is called fall. It is when the planet is placed in a sign opposing it's placement in dignity or exaltation. For instance, Venus is considered to be in dignity in Taurus or Libra, exaltation in Pisces and in fall in Scorpio and Aries. When Venus falls in Scorpio or Aries in the forensic chart it is considered to be peregrine. This renders it null and void. I never mention this placement in the analysis I post online because I just ignore the planet. No reason to go into it, really. So when you see this, you simply dismiss the planet, even if it rules an angle, and consider it to be weak and not active in the chart.

In this chart, Mercury is peregrine. It is placed in Pisces, where it is opposing it's natural placement in Virgo and is considered to be in fall in traditional astrology. You should dismiss Mercury in this chart for the most part.

How to Determine Planetary Motion

In the forensic chart, you are only interested in planetary motion for minutes or for hours. Daily motion usually plays no part except in the rare case where you end up charting for days on end, such as I did with the Caylee Anthony case. Most events in these cases are either stagnant, such as in the loss of an object, or moving over a few hours, as in an abuction, murder, lost child or pet. The rare case continues over days and even weeks if the subject is taken and still alive or you are tracking a runaway or lost pet.

You determine planetary motion over a few hours period by considering the hours in question and dividing the difference in motion by the hours. For instance, Mercury is at 12 degrees 15 minutes of Scorpio at 3 pm and then at 6 pm it is at 12 degrees 22 minutes of Scorpio. This is a motion of 7 minutes over a 3 hour period which averages down to 2 minutes an hour, 30 seconds every half hour or 1 second every minute. You will only need this if you are trying to pinpoint exactly when a specific aspect occurs and this will matter only when you are trying to pinpoint a moment in the event such as the exact moment of death or the exact moment when someone is attacked or taken. Again, this is rare but the need may arise at one time or another and you should know how to do it.

Locating Chart Rulers and Markers

First of all, the Moon is always the chart co ruler, regardless. If you are looking for a steady marker that will always play in the chart whether the other markers make sense or not, you can always go to the Moon. The house placement, sign placement and aspects of the Moon are extremely important in any and all forensic charts and should be considered first, even before other rulers and markers are found. In the sample chart, you can locate the Moon in Pisces in the fourth house.

The second most important ruler in any forensic chart is the first house ruler. This is the secondary marker for your subject, working with the Moon. In the sample chart, Scorpio is rising on the first house and it is ruled by Mars and Pluto. This makes Mars and Pluto the secondary rulers for your subject or victim. You can find Mars in Leo in the sample chart in the ninth house and Pluto in Sagittarius at the Ascendant. Because Pluto is at the first house cusp and it also co rules the first house, it is the single most powerful planet in this chart, even besides the Moon. And the fact that the Moon is sinister to a trine to Pluto makes this aspect the single most important aspect in the chart. You will want to watch this placement as you chart the case to see when it actually becomes exact. My guess is that this aspect will become exact (or perfect) in 6 hours but it still has great power in every minute inbetween then and now.

So now we know that the most important rulers for the subject are the Moon, Mars and Pluto, with Pluto taking the front seat. We can also call these markers.

The next important rulers or markers in the chart are those for the next person in the event, which is usually the abductor or rapist but can also be just people the subject interacts with. To determine the relationship between the subject and this person will be your biggest job. This person is ruled or marked by the seventh house and should always be considered the "next person" your subject will meet. Sometimes you will see one sign on the seventh house at one hour only to change very rapidly. Look closely at this to see if the first person wasn't someone who was just with your subject before the next person appeared.. and so on. The aspects that indicate abduction or assault are very definite and we will be looking for these later on. For now, you need to isolate the seventh house ruler and see if this ruler remains the same for awhile or changes quickly. In our sample chart, we have Taurus on the seventh house cusp and since Venus rules Taurus we need to find Venus in the chart. Venus is placed in the sign Pisces in the third house just outside the nadir. This is where the person she is about to meet is placed. You have to watch this placement closely in order to find out what happened.

So now we know that the Moon, Mars and Pluto mark our subject and that Venus marks the person she is about to meet. It will be up to you to determine if this person was her abductor or rapist or if this was just someone she knew that would be leaving the scene shortly. We see in the sample chart that the seventh house is in the last few degrees of Taurus so we will have to be careful in determining whether this subject left with this person or if someone else is coming along. This type of analysis takes some thinking ahead so I am going to give you a tip here. You can see that the next sign to move onto the seventh house is Gemini and this will happen within a half hour to an hour. Remember that Mercury, which rules Gemini, is peregrine and has no power in the chart. This, by itself, would make the current ruler, Venus, the permanent ruler for her abductor or rapist. This is because when the ruler changes signs it totally loses power and would be meaningless.

So we will take Taurus and Venus as the marker and ruler of the person who abducted this subject. But always remember that if the next sign and placement were to be a strong one, then the consideration remains that this first person could be anyone and the next person could be the abductor. Don't worry we will go over this again before we are done with the series.

Two other important markers or rulers are the tenth and fourth house placements. On the tenth we have the sign Virgo, which is ruled by Mercury. Again, Mercury is peregrine and powerless so we will dismiss the tenth house ruler. There are no planets in the tenth house to work as substitute markers so we will just dismiss the tenth house altogether in this analysis.

The fourth house is also an important marker in the chart as it rules the place where ths subject is at the hour in question. It also describes the home of the subject, the place from where she or he disappeared and the place to where he or she is headed. I know this sounds confusing but you use this house many times over during the course of the anlaysis. Here, the fourth house is housed by Pisces, though, and the ruler Neptunc is in Capricorn in the second house. The second house describes the subjects belongings. Because of this, we can assume that the fourth house is describing the subjects home, where she keeps her things. Neptune in Capricorn then becomes the marker for her home, the place from where she disappeared perhaps and this is the starting point for locating her later in the chart. That is a bit advanced for this portion of the learning process so we will save it for later. But just remember that the fourth house ruler is very important in any forensic chart and is a marker for several different things, including the home and current location.

Combining Planets and Houses in the Event Chart

This is one of the first steps in bringing the chart together. You have to combine the influences of the planets and houses in order to get the beginning of the picture. This is the first few pieces of the emerging puzzle. There are certain rules of thumb that you can use to get started but the real blending of these influences will come from you and your intuition. Let me give you a learning example from the sample chart.

The most important houses in the chart are always the angular houses, the first, fourth, seventh and tenth. Other houses that gain importance are those where angular rulers are placed. For example, Mars in Leo rules the first house and is placed in the ninth. This gives power to the ninth house. Venus in Taurus rules the seventh house and is placed in the third, so this placement gives the third house power in the chart. In determining action in the chart you always consider houses and planets. You only use the signs for descriptors and these are most often used in determining direction, descriptors for the players and locational markers. These will all be covered later on in the series so we will skip them for now. Now, we will concern ourselves with combining the influences of the planets and houses.

Let's take the first house ruler Mars in Leo in the ninth house. Mars rules the first house so we are using it as a marker for the subject or victim. The ninth house describes the outdoors and the woods but it also describes schools, universities, churchs, horse stables, army barracks, hunting lodges, sports arenas, campgrounds, long distance truckers and their trucks, garages, etc... there are many things the ninth house can implicate. Use your intuition and knowledge of the case to narrow down the possibilities. And what do we know about this case? We know that this child was found dead outside of an elementary school. She was outdoors and not inside the building. We can safely say that this marker is describing the victim on the school grounds, out in the open, as she was found. So we can feel pretty sure that this marker is spot on with the facts and can be safely used to mark our victim and follow her activities. This is a good example of how to blend the planets and the houses in the forensic chart.

Here are some rules of thumb to help you get started and to be used as a reference in the future as you work your way through the charts.

RULES OF THUMB: PLANETARY INFLUENCES IN ANGULAR HOUSES

FIRST HOUSE

The first house, the first house sign and it's ruler always mark the subject or victim. Here are the rules of thumb as it applies to planets in the first house.

1. The first house ruler in the first house shows the subject in their "own place" or a place where they normally feel safe.

2. The seventh house ruler in the first house shows the presence of someone else. Whether this is the abductor or murderer is for you to figure out. Most of the time it is.

3. The fourth house ruler in the first house shows the influence of the family or a family member in the event and can also show the subject in or around their own home.

4. The tenth house ruler in the first house shows the presence of someone who has influence over the subject, such as a boss, father figure, authority figure of some sort but can also show the authorities (the cops, for instance) on or around the scene.

5. Aggressive or chaotic planets like Mars, Pluto and Uranus in the first house often show unexpected events or acts of aggression.

6. The Moon in the first house has a similar meaning as the first house ruler in the first house.

7. Neptune in the first house almost always means a secret situation of some sort. The subject is either in hiding or being hidden. If Neptune also rules the seventh then this is a secret person, like a stalker, who is moving in on the victim. Neptune can also imply drug abuse or drunkenness so check the chart for supporting placements.

8. The fifth house ruler in the first house shows the presence of a child.

9. The eleventh house ruler in the first shows the presence of past partner of some sort. Most often this is an ex husband or wife; divorce is usually the state of the relationship.

10. The eighth house ruler in the first indicates the possible beginning of a death pattern. Saturn in the first can indicate the same thing. Check the chart for other placements.

FOURTH HOUSE

1. The first house ruler in the fourth house shows the victim or subject in their own home or near their own neighborhood.

2. The tenth house ruler in the fourth house shows the subject in a public establishment, usually a commercial one like a conveniance store, a nightclub or a library.. or any other place attended by the public.

3. The fourth house ruler in the fourth shows us the involvement of family in the situation as well as the family home or residence.

4. Fifth house ruler in the fourth house shows children in the subjects home.

5. The seventh house ruler in the fourth house shows someone entering the subjects home. Check other placements to determine if this was an invited guest or a break in.

6. The eighth house ruler is in the fourth house can show the beginning of a death pattern. Check other placements for a completion of this pattern.

7. The ninth house ruler in the fourth house can show the presence of a foreigner or person of a different culture in the subjects home. If the ninth house ruler accompanies the seventh house ruler in the fourth house then the person who has entered the home is probably of a different race or culture than the subject.

8. The eleventh house ruler in the fourth house can either show a visit from the ex husband or wife or can show a gathering of freinds in the subjects home. Check to see what applies.

9. The twelfth house ruler in the fourth can mean the beginning of a death pattern. Check the chart for completion of the pattern. Otherwise, it can also mean a funeral or burial.

10. The second house ruler in the fourth house can show a valuable item. This is probably something belonging to the subject and could have been stolen or may still be in the possession of the subject. Check to see what importance this item has.

SEVENTH HOUSE

1. The first house ruler in the seventh house shows the meeting between the subject and the other player in the event. Whether this is someone she has met to run away with or someone who has come along to harm her will be up to you to determine. It can describe the moment the abductor or murderer first arrived on the scene.

2. The tenth house ruler in the seventh house shows someone in authority on the scene. This usually means that the subject has met up with someone who is powerful and authoritarian.

3. The third house ruler in the seventh house or the seventh house ruler in the third shows that the subject knows the person he or she is with. This is either a neighbor, a sibling or an associate from school or work. They likely met up in the neighborhood. Also, the seventh house ruler in the third can show someone in a car or other vehicle.

4. The sixth house ruler in the seventh house shows that the place of employment is a factor in the meeting. Either the subject has met this person at a place they work or vice versa. The same thing applies if the seventh house ruler is in the sixth. In fact, when the seventh house ruler is in the sixth it shows the other person to actually be at work at the time.

5. The seventh house ruler in the eleventh house shows that the abductor or rapist was a friend of hers. This is someone she knew.

6. The seventh house ruler in the first shows a confrontation. She or he was surprised by the sudden appearance of this person.

7. The seventh house ruler in the fourth house shows someone entering the subjects home. The seventh house ruler in the tenth house shows the meeting happened in a public place.

8. The seventh house ruler in the second house shows a robbery. The person may have come along in order to take something from the subject. Also, the second house ruler in the seventh shows the other person to still be in possession of something belonging to the victim.

9. The seventh house ruler in the eighth house describes a criminal or a sleazy, scary person. This person is very dangerous.

10. The seventh house ruler in the fifth house can mean that the other person is a child or young person. It can also describe a rape if the other aspects fit.

TENTH HOUSE

1. The tenth house ruler in the first house shows the presence of someone powerful. Most often this is a father figure with influence over the subject.

2. The first house ruler in the tenth house shows that the subject was the one in a position of power. Perhaps he or she is a supervisor on their job or holds a public office. It can often mean that they are in the company of an employee or dependant. Check the chart for other indicators.

3. The third house ruler in the tenth can mean the subject is looking for a ride; can mean she or he is hitchhiking. They are out in the open, probably along a highway somewhere.

4. The eighth house ruler in the tenth house can describe rape in a public place. If it is a part of a death pattern, then consider that the subject died or was murdered in a public place.

5. The eleventh house ruler in the tenth house can mean the subject is with a friend who has great influence over their life. This can also mean that the subject has run off to fulfill a dream or wish.

6. The ninth house ruler in the tenth house or conjunct the midheaven can show the subject in the company of foreigners. The tenth house ruler in the ninth can also show the subject in school or on school grounds. It might also mean the subject is in court or in jail. Either placement can also mean the subject has gone on a trip and can also mean he or she has gotten on a plane. The subject may have left the country. The chart will have to offer other descriptors.

7. The sixth house ruler in the tenth house shows the subject having a concern about work or health. With the tenth house ruler in the sixth house, hey may work in the health care industry. Sometimes this placement means the subject went to a job interview before they went missing. Sometimes it means they disappeared from their job site.

8. The twelfth house ruler in the tenth house can mean burial in a public place. The body may be out in the open.

9. The tenth house ruler in the twelfth house can mean that someone is keeping a secret about the whereabouts of the subject. Most often this is someone who is important in the life of the subject. Sometimes this means that one of the parents is hiding something.

10. The fourth house ruler or first house ruler in the tenth house can show the subject in the home of the abductor. If Saturn is nearby or has power in the chart, consider they are being held against their will. The sign on the midheaven can help you figure out where that location may be.

THERE ARE TO BE CONSIDERED RULES OF THUMB AS YOU WORK ON YOUR ANALYSIS BUT THEY ARE STILL FLEXIBLE AND CAN BE INFLUENCED BY OTHER PLACEMENTS. USE THEM WITH CARE.

Determining Dispositions

This is actually much easier than it seems. It is one of the most important determinants in the chart so you have to get good at it. Planets are disposed of by the planets that rule the sign they are in. For instance, Venus rules Taurus so any planet in Taurus is disposed of by Venus.

Dispositions give the disposition of the placement and will give you the reasons behind the actions you see in the chart. I will use a complicated scenario to help you understand the scope of the disposition. In our sample chart, the seventh house ruler is Venus and you can consider this to be the marker for the person our subject met up with. This could be her abductor or killer. We see that Venus is in the third house so perhaps this person is in a car or vehicle or perhaps they are in the subjects car? We can see that Venus is in Pisces so the marker for the abductor is Venus in Pisces. Venus is disposed of by Neptune because Neptune rules Pisces. Locate Neptune in the chart and you can see what the abductor is up to.

In our sample chart, Neptune is in Capricorn in the second house. This shows the abductor to be interested in something the victim had. Either this person was trying to steal something from her or was interested in keeping something of hers, perhaps as a trophy. But seeing that the marker is Neptune, which is known for hidden things and secrets, we might assume he was sneaking around trying to get something without being seen. In fact, Neptune is in Capricorn so we can think that what he was after was something of value. It may even have been a heirloom or other valuable family item. We say this because of what we know about the nature of Capricorn.

So you can see here how we can figure out the motives behind the actions by using dispositions. In this case, I would guess that the abductor went through her car in order to find something he considered valuable or desirable. So from this alone we get the feeling that the abductor knew his victim before he killed her. Knew her well enough to be after her things.

Part Six: Exercises in Forensic Astrology
Section One: Practice Session

The first thing I want you to do is draw up your own forensic chart. It will be up to you to select a case that interests you and to gather the information you need for a viable chart. Remember that not every case will have all the information you need so choose several charts to work with. Once you have the time, date and location where the subject was last seen, when the dog was first discovered missing, when the child last left home, etc... then you should be able to draw up a forensic chart. If you cannot do this by hand or have no personal method for doing so, go to http://www.astrolabe.com/freechart. Fill in the information you have for the case in question and submit. Your chart will appear if the information is complete and correct.

Once you have the chart, save it to your hard drive so you can access it later.

Step One: QUIZ: Creating the Chart

Before you draw up the chart, here are the questions I want you to answer:

1. What kind of case am I working on?

2. Is there a dead body or a known time of death?

3. What is the time at which the subject was last seen or heard from? Or what was the time when the body was discovered? Or what was the time the coroner gave for probable time of death? The first question must be answered in every case but the next two only apply in cases where the body has been found but the killer is still at large.

4. At what location did the subject disappear from? At what location was the body found? Do you have more than one location in this case? In other words, was the subject last seen in one place and then seen again in another? You will have to draw up charts for both locations at the applicable date and location. This is also true if the subject was last seen in one location and then the body was found later in another location. Both charts have to be drawn and ultimately compared for analysis.

4. What was the date when the subject went missing or when the body was found? Does this case include more than one day? In other words, on what date did the subject disappear and is this different that the day they were found, if they were found? If the subject went missing in one location at a certain time and then was found in the same location at a different time, dead or alive, charts will have to be drawn for both times at the same location and compared for analysis.

5. What was the subject doing when they were last heard from or seen? Were there other people with the subject at the time? This information is very useful but not necessary to the analysis. Try to get this if you can. This is very useful in helping you determine the viability of the chart.

Step Two: QUIZ: Making Sense of the Chart

Step Two starts with determining viability. Answer the following questions to determine if the chart you have is readable.

1. Is the time close to midnight or noon? Will I need charts for more than one day? If so, you will need to run charts for subsequent hours and sometimes this can include days. If the time they went missing was close to midnight, please remember to move the dates forward as you run charts for the subsequent morning.

2. What is the sign on the first house cusp? In what degree is the sign placed? Signs in the very first two degrees and the last two degrees create difficult charts that are often not readable. You will have to inspect these charts more closely than others. But either way continue with the determination questions to see if the chart will work.

Step Three: QUIZ: Beginning the Analysis

1. What is the ruler of the sign on the first house cusp? This planet will be the marker for your subject. For instance, if Aries is on the first house cusp then Mars will be the marker for your subject.

2. Where in the chart do you find the marker? In what house? For example, if Mars rules the first house then you must locate Mars in the chart. Once you do, you are looking at your subject. Don't forget that.

3. If the marker is in an angular house (first, fourth, seventh or tenth house) then they are in a powerful position at the time. In other houses, not so much. Make note of the house and sign the marker is in.

4. In charts where the subject was last seen and is still missing, ompare your notes with what is known about the last sighting and see if it fits what you see in the chart. For instance, you are told that the subject was last seen leaving school. You find that the first house ruler is in the ninth house, which is traditional marker for schools. You would say the chart is probably viable, even if the degree on the first house cusp is very early or late.

5. In charts where the dead body was located and this is the time you are using, then compare the placement of the marker in the chart with what you know about the body discovery. For instance, if the body was found buried in the woods and the first house marker is in the ninth house, a traditional marker for the woods, you would then say the chart is probably viable.

6. If there are different times for different sightings involved in the case, you will have to do the same comparisons on every chart. Starting with the place and time they were last seen or the body was discovered. For instance, if the subject was last seen in a particular time and place and the chart for that time and place appears to be viable, comparisons should be made to any charts where she or he was seen again at a later date or when the body was discovered. See if these charts are viable as well. This should be done for the time of body discovery for sure no matter what. If the body is found on a city street and the markers show a neighborhood or avenue then you would say that this chart was viable, too.

There are always exceptions to every rule, so I will add this. If the chart for the time last seen is a good one but then the chart for a time of a later sighting doesn't fit, I would double check the source on the second sighting and discard the chart if it seems questionable. If you can work with the chart for the time last seen then do so in every instance. Do not allow other charts to distract you. But if you have a viable chart for the last sighting and then the chart for the body discovery does not work, then further investigation must be done. If you cannot make these charts work together you will to discard the case. Take my word for it. If the chart for time of death does not work with the chart for the time last seen the charts are not viable.

Charts are not viable if you cannot read them. It's as simple as that.

SECTION TWO: TRACKING MOVEMENTS IN THE FORENSIC CHART

FORWARD

Having accurate event times and tracking movements from one minute to the next is an important part of my method of forensic analysis. In fact, for me, the forensic chart is about tracking movements over time in order to determine the outcome of events and sometimes these events occur over days at a time, requiring charts to be done hour by hour over a period of time. There are often multiple events within a singular event, including the time when the subject was last seen, the time when the subject was found dead, the time when the subject's car is located, etc... and all of this has to be woven together into the tale that is told by the charts you are creating and reading. And many of these events within the main event occur over a period of days, weeks or months.

This is an important step in the process of building a forensic analysis. Once you have isolated chart rulers and their influence in the chart, you then must learn to track their movements in the chart and give every event an average window of time. Although time in space is different than arbitrary time on this planet, adjustments can be made to center the two. This is only possible to accomplish because we are actually standing on the Earth here and now and not some distance away. The farther away you are from the planet's surface, the farther back time tracks. This is science. And knowing that, I have always wondered that if you moved closer to the center of the Earth could you not move into the future? Just some groovy food for thought.

Meditations on earth science aside, I am going to try to help you pinpoint time in the charts you are analyzing and track the movements of the planets through that window of time. You will never be exact, so you need to get that out of your head right away or you will go crazy trying. But the variables can be narrowed down to where you are very close. In most events where a forensic chart is used, the exact time and place of the last sighting or the eye witness account of an actual occurrence can be used as a moment in time spanning the entire time in question. Many charts drawn for the first time known can tell the entire story, from start to finish. But depending on how far out your event goes, this can get hazy. In the Caylee Anthony case, for instance, it had been said that the child was in the trunk of the car, which the charts supported. But this was over a long period of time, just over a month, so the chart drawn for the time when the child was last seen stopped giving information after a day or two. In that case, recorded cell phone pings were used to track the movements of her mother, Casey, to determine what actually was going on. But in most cases, where someone is abducted and murdered within a few hours, the orignal event chart will tell you everything.

I want you to use a new chart for this purpose and discard the Deanna Cremin charts I had you use in the first book. The reason for this is because there was no transport of Deanna's body and there was no more movement between her and her killer. She was killed very near to where she was last seen and her body was not moved. So in this instance, I want you to use a chart that has more movement in it to study. This would be the charts for the Lauren Spierer abduction case. I want you to use the chart shown below as the starter chart for the case and run charts of your own as you move the case forward. Don't worry I will show you how to do that as we go along.

DETERMINING STARTING POINTS AND LOCATIONS

Discovering Starting Locations

This can be an important detail in any analysis. It is important in determining, for instance, what exactly transpired between a victim and their killer, where the person was taken after the abduction and where the person may have been killed if they were indeed murdered. This can help in locating the murder location if it is unknown. But it's best and most desired use is in locating unfound bodies. When you can start by pinpointing a direction in which the body was taken, it is often only the identification of markers from there on. The combination of directions and isolating these landscape markers that allow the analyst to give an idea of where the body might be found. So let's concentrate on determininng directions and we will start by using the Spierer case as an example.

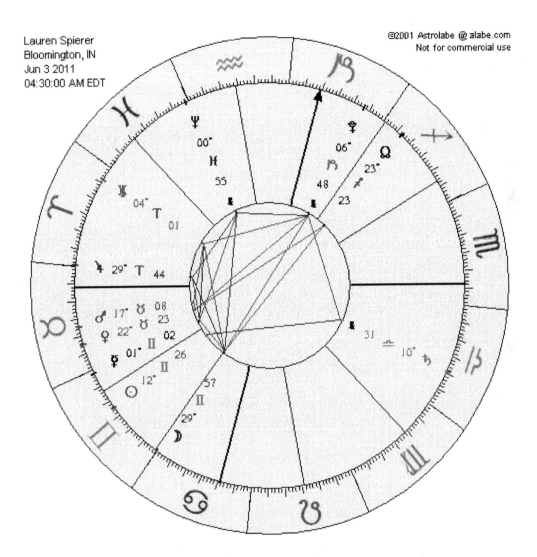

This is an identical copy of the same event chart I presented in the analysis on the blog. I want to use it this time to explain how directions are discovered in the forensic chart. This practice is based on traditional astrological teachings for the directions indicated by houses and planets.

I use these traditional teachings in my work but sometimes have to blend opposing influences to come up with a reasonable directional assessment. I will show you what I mean.

First, some background on the Spierer case.

BLOOMINGTON, Ind. - Eleven years after an Indiana University student disappeared while on a bike ride, the scene in this college town is eerily similar, with parents and volunteers frantically searching for another missing woman with no sign of what happened to her.

Police they say they have few leads and no suspects but believe foul play is to blame for the disappearance of 20-year-old Lauren Spierer, a petite sophomore from Greenburgh, N.Y., last seen leaving a friend's apartment early Friday after a night out.

"When somebody at 4:30 in the morning — no shoes and has earlier been drinking — goes out and just disappears off a street corner, we feel like there certainly could be foul play involved," Bloomington police Lt. Bill Parker said during a news conference Tuesday. "If she had just decided to go to a buddy's house, we would have heard that by now."

Foul play possible in Spierer case, say cops

Police looking for clues about Spierer used a battering ram to break into the security room and mail room at her apartment building Tuesday evening, according to WTHR-TV and WISH-TV reporters at the scene. Bloomington police declined comment, saying they planned to issue a statement Wednesday morning. But the apartment complex issued a statement indicating police were after computer hard drives and no one was available to let officers into the locked area.

Parker said Spierer went to a sports bar near her apartment with friends Thursday night, then went to a friend's apartment before leaving around 4:30 a.m. Friday. Her friend watched Spierer walk to a corner near his apartment, but no one has seen her since.

Investigators have Spierer's purse and some keys, which were found along the route to her friend's apartment. But Parker said they aren't sure whether Spierer left them on her way to or from her friend's home. She left her cellphone and shoes in the bar.

Authorities directing volunteers have told them to look for clues — a stray piece of clothing left on the ground or anything that raises suspicion. Fliers with Spierer's photograph and a physical description of her are posted around Bloomington and on the Indiana University campus.

Bloomington residents say they hope for a better outcome in the Spierer case than the Behrman case, which dragged on for years.

"Those people went through such a terrible, terrible time," said Sharon Phillips, a Bloomington resident with two adult daughters who volunteered with the search Tuesday. "It's heart-wrenching. Anyone's who's a parent is just going to have that kind of a connection to these people."

Robert Spierer, meanwhile, begged for anyone with any information about his daughter's disappearance to come forward.

"It doesn't matter how casual the sighting was. Every little piece of info we get is important," he said.

From ABC News: 'The search for the missing Indiana University student has encountered an unusual hurdle. One of the last people to see her alive claims he is suffering from memory loss.

Two hours before Spierer vanished, surveillance cameras captured her coming from Kilroy Sports Bar back to her apartment building with a friend, Corey Rossman. The cameras captured a scuffle between Rossman and another young man at the Smallwood Plaza apartment building complex.

"He was punched in the face. We don't know who, why or what was said, but that punch or punches caused him a temporary memory loss," said Carl Satzmann, Rossman's attorney.

Spierer and Rossman left the apartment building and she escorted Rossman back to his apartment. She was there for about an hour with Rossman and another young man.

Rossman doesn't remember Spierer walking him back to his apartment and the first thing he remembers is waking up the next morning, his attorney said. Police have searched Rossman's car and cell phone.

After returning Rossman to his apartment, Spierer left for another friend's apartment. That friend saw her walk towards her own apartment at about 4:30 a.m. last Friday. The pint-sized student who weighs less than 100 pounds and is 4-foot-11 was last seen three blocks from her apartment.

Surveillance video also shows Lauren in an alley walking with an acquaintance on the morning she disappeared. The alley is the same place where her keys and coin purse were found by authorities.

==
TRADITIONAL DIRECTIONS BY HOUSE
==

FIRST HOUSE - *EAST*
SECOND HOUSE - *NORTH BY EAST*
THIRD HOUSE - *NORTHEAST*
FOURTH HOUSE - *NORTH*
FIFTH HOUSE - *NORTH BY WEST*
SIXTH HOUSE - *NORTHWEST*
SEVENTH HOUSE - *WEST*
EIGHTH HOUSE - *SOUTH BY WEST*
NINTH HOUSE - *SOUTHWEST*
TENTH HOUSE - *SOUTH*
ELEVENTH HOUSE - *SOUTHEAST BY SOUTH*
TWELFTH HOUSE - *EAST SOUTHEAST*

==
TRADITIONAL DIRECTIONS BY SIGN
==

ARIES - *EAST*
TAURUS - *SOUTH BY EAST*
GEMINI - *WEST BY SOUTH*
CANCER - *NORTH*
LEO - *EAST BY NORTH*
VIRGO - *SOUTH BY WEST*
LIBRA - *WEST*
SCORPIO - *NORTH BY EAST*
SAGITTARIUS - *EAST BY SOUTH*
CAPRICORN - *SOUTH*
AQUARIUS - *WEST BY NORTH*
PISCES - *NORTH BY WEST*

==

Using this table, you can begin to decipher directions in the forensic chart. However, this won't be the final word on it's own. It will take practice, insight and judgement on your part to blend the various influences in the chart to determine what may be the true direction. This determination is used often in forensic charts, to determine which direction the abductor may have gone after taking his victim, which direction the murderer traveled with the body, in which direction one should look to find the body and what direction the runaway child or pet may have taken when leaving the home area. So this is an important and valuable determination you will be asked to make when doing forensic charts for clients and friends.

As I said, it is nearly impossible to make a clean determination from just the traditional directions. Let me explain why. Taking our example chart (above) let's say we want to know what direction the victim was traveling in. This is the first chart available, the one for the time when she was last seen. The murderer has not arrived yet and she is still alive. We know that she is represented by both Venus in Taurus in the first house and the Moon in Gemini in the third house. We know this because Taurus is on the first house cusp, which makes Venus her ruler, and in every event chart, the Moon presides as chart co ruler. The third house describes any vehicle she may have been driving and the fourth shows us her own home neighborhood. The first house is ruled by Taurus, which is directional south by west and the fourth house is ruled by Cancer, which is north. From these placements, assuming the victim to be stagnant at this moment, we can say that she is moving around in a southwesterly direction and that her actual home is north of here. And yet it will not be this simple, as you will soon see.

Other markers for the direction she may have traveled are found by closer examination of her planetary markers. The third house shows us the actual direction she traveled in. Moon in Gemini supports the claim that she was "on the move" or had left the location she had been at previously. Moon in Gemini is disposed of by Mercury, which is in Gemini in the first house. This is a marker for directional east. Also, this is a marker for her own neighborhood, or someplace very close to where she lived. The Venus in Taurus in the first disposes of itself so from this we can assume that she is moving under her own volition and was not coerced or forced. Any time a planet disposes of itself it shows tremendous strength and power and when planets are placed in the first house, whether in dignity or not, they usually show self determination and control. So she is moving along, at this time, because she had decided to do so. But the preponderance of important planets in the first house, including the chart ruler and the third house ruler, as well, I would venture to guess that she was traveling east from her original location. Or, at best, this is what the charts appear to tell us. This will have to be compared with known facts.

With this information, we have been able to determine the starting point for this event. She is in a neighborhood near her own home, moving on foot in an easterly direction from an area in a southwest location from the city center.

Other factors may have to be considered in cases where you are trying to nail down more complex movements, whether it be unknown starting points or movement as the event unfolds. Although we were able to determine a directional startingn point for the victim in this case, we haven't even begun to touch the more important aspects, which will be movement and direction surrounding the actual abduction and murder. To do these kinds of calculations, you will need a ton of information to work with. Starting with the places and things defined by signs, houses and planets. Once you have this information, you should be able to single out certain features in the landscape, for instance, or to determine whether a body was buried or dumped in the water. Study these charts and try your best to get a sense of what each planet, sign and house can indicate in the real world.

Signs: Places and Things

<u>ARIES:</u>

Places: Sandy and hilly ground, newly built land or where construction work is taking place. All places where the land has been recently dug up, whether for farming or for development. Land where sheep and small cattle feed or stables for small animals. Unfrequented places where criminals find refuge such as abandoned houses turned into crackhouses or hideouts for fugitives.

Inside the home, it can describe the ceiling and the plastering or covering of the house. As a fire sign Aries can indicate places near fire or sources of heat, such as outside and inside fireplaces and furnaces; chimneys.

In general public locations it can indicate laboratories, especially those where chemicals are boiled or distilled. Also dentist offices, barber shops and locksmiths, where sharp instruments and heat are often used. Also distilleries and canneries; bakery shops or pizza shops (where large ovens or kilns are in use); tool shops (sharp, cutting tools) and smelters and brick foundaries with visible fire. Also butcher shops and slaughterhouses.

Countries & cities: Include England, Germany, France, Sweden, Poland, Denmark, Palestine, Syria; Florence, Naples, Marseilles.

Colours: Hot, fiery or burnt colours. Red in particular and also hot pink.

Stones & Metals: Stones and metals fall under the rulership of planets, not signs, but through its association with Mars, Aries has affinity with bloodstone, jasper, and vermilion.

Direction: East

TAURUS:

Places: Stables where horses and cattle or their implements are kept. Farm land or pasture land away from housing estates. Low houses (bungalows, cottages), or in houses, low rooms or cellars. As an earth sign Taurus indicates places low down, near the floor. Can also describe wheatfields, gardens, trees (near a house) and cow pastures. In general areas, it describes a beautifully manicured park, for instance, that is small in size with no water source but abounding in small, slow moving ground animals like turtles and snails. Overall, it rules well tended gardens with blooming flowers like poppies, daisies and violets as well as public gardens.

Describes businesses related to value and/or luxury so it can indicate banks or expensive hotels. Taurus also describes beauty salons, spas, gyms, massage parlors and high priced call girls.

Inside the house, Taurus can describe dark closets, floorboards, storage for heavy dark clothing (especially wool), safes, trunks and heavy wood furniture. Also the places where wood furniture may be stored. Places where money is kept such as purses and lockboxes. It can also indicate places where food is stored, especially the lower shelves and floor of the pantry. Jewelry boxes and floor safes. Also the lowest rooms in the house, especially the basement and especially so if food or valuables are stored there.

Countries & cities: Include Poland, northern part of Sweden, Russia, Ireland, Switzerland, northern Italy, Persia, Cyprus, Iran. Lorraine and Nantes in France; Parma, Bologna, Palermo, Mantua, Sienna and Brescia in Italy; Karlstad in Sweden, Novgorod in Russia; Wurzburg, and Leipzig in Germany.

Colours: Earthy colours. Brown, terracota, beige - but green in particular. Sometimes a lemony white color.

Stones & Metals: Stones and metals fall under the rulership of planets, not signs, but the emerald is often linked to Taurus because of its green colour. Through its association with Venus, Taurus has affinity with Copper, marcasite, alabaster, lapis lazuli and chrysolite

Direction: South by East (southeast)

GEMINI

Places: As an air sign, Gemini describes hills and mountains. Gemini has affinity for the planet Mercury so it also rules barns and storehouses for corn and grain. Outdoors, it relates to tennis and badminton courts, mailboxes, mail depots and garages. Public places where cars are allowed, most especially those places that they are usually not. Small winding roads along sparsely populated areas; one lane neighborhood roads in residential areas; the storage shed in the back yard or shared by many; the neighborhood park where kids congregate, perhaps using swings or flying kites. Areas populated with small animals that use their hands and live in trees such as opossum, squirrels and raccoons. Areas with lots of birds.

Inside the house it describes libraries and studies (with books and bookcases), the walls of houses (especially those that have been papered or otherwise decorated), the hall, playrooms and game rooms. Can also describe chests, drawers, coffers and places where money is stored or kept, *ie*, treasuries, purses. As an air sign Gemini relates to places off the ground, high up (such as upstairs rooms) or near sources of light, such as windows or rooms that are notably light, bright and 'airy'.

Can also indicate schools, nurseries, public garages, cell phone towers, lookouts on mountaintops (such as ranger stations), attorneys offices and golf courses.

Countries & cities: Include Italy, Belgium, Armenia. The west and southwest of England, London, Louvain in France, Bruges in Belgium; Nuremburg, Hassfurt, Mainz and Bamberg in Germany; Cordova in Spain, Cesena in Italy.

Colours: Mixed colours. Often associated with yellow, or yellowish green. Also a very light pink, such as crimson mixed with white.

Stones & Metals: Stones and metals fall under the rulership of planets, not signs, but through its association with Mercury, Gemini is often linked with agate, quicksilver and stones of diverse colours.

Direction: West by South

CANCER

Places: Cancer is a water sign and it rules places where water is present. Cancer rules the crab so these are bodies of water that are a little more shallow than those of Pisces (fish) and a bit deeper than those of Scorpio (cesspools and ponds). Cancer can indicate the sea (the ocean) but it most often describes rivers and smaller, more local sources of deeper water such as ponds, brooks, springs, wells, wash-houses, sea shores, marshy land, etc. Can also indicate hydrants and reservoirs or retention ponds. Often means fast moving water (from the rulership of the Moon), such as rushing rivers or bubbling brooks but can also describe very deep, still lakes and ponds. Also refers to the ocean, with both the fast moving waves and deep waters. Consider beaches, bath houses near the beach and muddy waters near the shoreline. In general, I consider Cancer to refer to deeper, mid-sized bodies of water and no so much the puddles and bogs (more often ruled by Scorpio)..

In houses it represents cellars, cisterns, bathrooms and sinks. Can include areas where liquids are kept, especially cabinets in bathrooms which contain liquids and chemicals. It also describes the kitchen, the laundry and the general plumbing in the house. Can refer to hydrants just outside the home, water outlets on the building, retention ponds adjacent to the home or building, the backyard swimming pool or lake. Also sinkholes under and around the home.

Homes on the waterfront, including canal systems as well as ocean or lakefront. Rules public parks with bodies of water such as ponds or lakes. Also public swimming pools.

Countries & cities: Include Scotland, Holland, Tunisia, Algeria, Istanbul, Venice, Milan, Amsterdam, York, Wittenburg in Germany, Cadiz in Spain.

Colors: Pale, discreet and subtle colours; greys, beiges, silver, white. Also a bluish or brownish green.

Stones & Metals: Stones and metals fall under the rulership of planets, not signs, but through its association with the Moon, Cancer has affinity with pearls, silver and crystals

Direction: North

LEO

Places: All 'majestic' and grandly furnished places such as theatres, lavish public buildings and monuments. Especially elegant or lavish buildings associated with government. Also public halls, auditoriums and amusement parks. Leo also rules places connected with royalty and principle rulers: palaces, castles, forts. Conversely, it also indicates inaccessible places such as deserts, forests and areas where wild animals (large ones usually) roam freely. Can indicate a heavily forested area, a jungle and/or the deep, dark woods. Sometimes refers to a heavily forested public park.

Inside houses Leo signifies places near to sources of heat and fire such as chimneys, or areas where the furnishings are particularly grand and rich. Usually indicates a closet filled with plush velvets and silks in dramatic colours with sequins, glitter and other gilt ornaments. Traditionally refers to dens and bedrooms. Also man caves and game rooms, the party area of the home.

In public areas, Leo often indicates government buildings, dance halls or ballrooms, nightclubs (with entertainment), gambling casinos and places of amusement. Can refer to places where children gather to play games, including playgrounds and video game rooms. In general, Leo rules entertainers and performers of all kinds, including freak shows and local bands.

Countries & cities: Include Italy, Rome, the Alps; the Czech Republic, Turkey, Sicily, Prague, Alsace in France, Damascus, Lintz in Austria, Coblenz in Germany, Bristol in England.

Colours: Yellow, red and orange, gold and rich, deep and vibrant 'royal' colours. Also bright green.

Stones & Metals: Stones and metals fall under the rulership of planets, not signs, but through its association with the Sun, Leo has affinity with gold, rubies, cats eyes, diamonds, dark red garnets and lustrous orange-yellow, orange-red, or yellow-brown zircon stones.

Direction: East by North

VIRGO

Places: Like all the earth signs, Virgo governs places that are low down and near to the floor. It also rules places connected with agriculture, harvest and agricultural storage, in particular dairies, granaries, malt-houses (and breweries), cornfields, hay-racks, greenhouses, places connected to barley, wheat or peas or where cheese and butter is churned or stored. Chicken ranches.

Inside the house it signifies areas and objects used for study, accountancy, or storage; the former includes libraries, book cases, or places where books, pens and reading/writing instruments are kept, (typewriters, word processors and computers), study halls, office areas and items used for book-keeping. The latter includes cupboards, pantries, closets, cabinets, drawers, small compartments, medicine cupboards (and drug stores generally through its association with health). Also is affiliated with writing studios and warehouses or storehouses for large amounts of groceries.

Virgo will also signify objects or areas that serve a purely utilitarian purpose - places or things that are used to store, restore, or repair, such as sewing instruments and machines (also knitting and spinning equipment), tools, and servants quarters in homes that have them.

Modern authors associate the sign with places connected with pets, small animals and veterinary services.

Countries & cities: Include Turkey, Southern Greece, Athens, Iraq, Baghdad, Croatia, Africa, Jerusalem, South-west France, Toulouse, Paris, Lyons, Rhodes, Heidelburg in Germany, Basle in Switzerland, and Brindisi in Italy.

Colours: Lilly associates Virgo with the colour black speckled with blue. Other authors have associated it with white. In general Virgos avoid strong dynamic colours in decor and personal attire, preferring subtle hues and muted greys and earthy tones.

Stones & Metals: Stones and metals fall under the rulership of planets, not signs, but through its association with Mercury, Virgo is often linked with agate, sardonyx and stones of diverse colours. Agate seems particularly suitable, since its metaphysical property is said to aid digestion and offer eloquence in writing.

Direction: South by West (southwest)

LIBRA

Places: As an air sign, Libra governs places that are exposed to wind and air and/or high off the ground. Outdoors, this includes places where the air is fresh and cool, such as on mountains and along hillsides. It also rules windmills and places that deal with the processing of wind power. Traditionally it is said to rule places where birds are hunted (those that fly) and where hawking is practiced, whether in sport or for entertainment. Libra also rules flying and floating objects, such as balloons, planes and missiles and rules air force bases, airports, and high communication towers. Because Libra is known to rule tall trees in open spaces, it is also given rulership over sandy and gravely ground, saw-pits, lumber mills, places where wood is cut or stored, and to barns or out-houses that lie away from other dwellings.

Libra is also considered to represent weapons that fly through the air, such as bows and arrows and bullets. Sagittarius also has some affinity with bows and arrows and ammunition as well. However, Libra most often describes a knife, something light with a sharp blade, even where other air signs may not. The presence of Libra as angular in a body locator chart is a clue that the body may be out in the open (exposed to air) on a hillside or on top of a mountain. Don't forget the sandy ground.

Inside buildings, Libra indicates places near windows or off the floor towards the ceiling, such as attics, ventilation ducts, the upper rooms in houses, garrets, chambers and rooms that lie inside others, such as walk-in wardrobes. Libra is most often associated with upstairs bedrooms and attics, especially where family momentos are stored.

Countries & cities: Include the higher regions of Austria, Alsace and Arles in France, Estonia and Latvia, Lisbon in Portugal, Frankfort and Spires in Germany, Vienna, Thebes in Greece and Fribourg in Switzerland.

Colours The colours of Libra are those that are not excessive in shade or hue. Greys, pastels, and subtle tones. Also commonly describes black (which is the ultimate non color) or a brick red (russet) which can be dull and subtle.

Stones & Metals: Stones and metals fall under the rulership of planets, not signs, but through its association with Venus, Libra has affinity with copper, sapphires, marcasite, lapis lazuli and chrysolite

Direction: West

SCORPIO

Places: Because Scorpio is ruled by disruptive Mars and the chaotic Pluto, many of the places it rules suggest a hostile environment. These are places that seem threatening, may cause fear, especially those that are dark and difficult to navigate. These types of places would include areas where there are rats or snakes, crocodiles, komodos (or other large lizards) and/or an area teeming with insects. Scorpio defines those places that are dark and dirty. It also depicts places that are filled with grief and mourning, such as funeral parlors, graveyards, cemetaries, etc.. In general, Scorpio rules vaults (and other places where people or things are locked up and hidden), sewers, plumbing, sinks, toilets (indoor- Libra rules outhouses), marshes, vineyards, stagnant pools and almost any location that smells badly. Because it is a fixed water sign, Scorpio describes all locations where water collects and stagnates. This can mean muddy or swampy grounds, bogs, marshes, sedimentary deposits, cesspools, sewer runoff or sludge and quagmires. (A perfect example being a boggy area with lots of mosquitos and snakes). Can also refer to areas that are flooded, underwater for long periods, torrential rains and areas where the sun never shines (Alaska part of the year and Seattle a lot of the time).

Inside the house Scorpio points most often to sinks, toilets, sewer drains, plumbing, medicine cabinets and vaults. Any place in the room where water is leaking in or gathering. Consider also cabinets where toxic chemicals are kept, the cellar, pantries and larders that are cold and dark (especially those with insects as well), the unfinished basement, any part of the home that is unfinished and standing in disarray, decaying areas of the home, black mold, cockroaches, and any area of the home that has been left empty or in disrepair and is in need or renovation or demolition. Scorpio also indicates any areas that are cold and dark, low down or underground, or near water used to eliminate waste. Also depicts furniture and artefacts made from clay.

In the garden Scorpio will represent muddy areas, compost heaps, the sunless north-facing wall, inaccessible areas, pot holes, puddles and stagnant ponds. Any area outdoors or around the home that is insect infested, marshy, sinking, has stagnant pools of water or overgrown with weeds and other noxious plants. A vineyard if present.

Countries & cities: Include Northern Bavaria, Norway, Algeria, Morocco, Catalonia and Valencia in Spain, Urbrino, Messina and Frejus in Italy, Vienne in France, Ghent in Belgium, and Frankfurt in Germany.

Colours: Generally defined as brown, although sometimes described as dark red, grey red or black red, from which we can assume a dark, blood-red brown.

Stones & Metals: Stones and metals fall under the rulership of planets, not signs, but through its association with Mars, Scorpio is often linked with iron, ocre, bloodstone, jasper, red lead or vermilion.

Direction: North by East (northeast)

SAGITTARIUS

Places: As a fire sign, Sagittarius governs places that are exposed to heat or fire. This can literally mean houses and buildings that have been burnt to the ground. Also outside grills, indoor fireplaces, crematoriums, any cooking pan meant to be used over open fire. It can mean the body was burned after death. Smoke pits in the ground, cast iron cookware, stand alone smokers, places where the forestry service has done burnoff. Through its affinity with horses it also rules stables (in particular military stables or stables where important commercial horses are kept). Also horse slaughterhouses and the caging for wild horses kept by the Bureau of Land Management. Outside it represents upper areas on the landscape, open fields, hills and land that rises higher than the rest. It will usually mark an area with high sloping ground but not as high or vast as mountains or hillsides.

Inside it indicates the upper rooms, particularly near the hearth or fireplace, usually where there is an expansive feeling of space. Sagittarius generally rules the largest areas of the house, where there is lots of room. Large patio areas with attached gardens and/or ornamental gathering places such as tiki bars and fire pits. It also rules the chimney and most especially fireplaces in upper rooms. Rooftop grills or other sources of heat.

Sagittarius also rules Army barracks and places where ammunition is stored, especially bullets. It has an affinity for bows and arrows and people who travel on horseback.

Countries & cities: Include Spain (especially Toledo), Hungary (especially Budapest), Slavonia, Croatia, the Czech Republic, Narbonne and Cologne in France.

Colours: The colours of Sagittarius are bright and vivid, including red, purple and royal blue. Lilly assigns a mixture of yellow and green (turquoise), whilst sea-green, blue, and purple are particularly emphasised through the rulership of Jupiter. Objects in the area that are bright yellow or a sanguine green.

Stones & Metals: Stones and metals fall under the rulership of planets, not signs, but through its association with Jupiter, Sagittarius has affinity with tin, amethysts, saphires, emeralds, crystals, topaz and marble.

Direction: East by South

CAPRICORN

Places: As an earth sign Capricorn signifies places where people work the Earth. This would include farms, farming equipment, wood stores and places where farm animals roam. Through it's rulership by Saturn, Capricorn specifically rules over fallow land, barren fields, land that is bushy and thorny, or where there are dunghills, compost heaps or soil prepared with animal manure. Like all earth signs it indicates locations that are low down, either near or on the ground. It particularly signifies low dark places. This would most often be a low dark corner of the home or the threshold under the entrance. In general, Capricorn rules prisons, churchyards, tombs, urns, snow sheds and dark, cold, empty areas on the first floor. In daily life, Capricorn indicates the business district of the city, city hall, the chamber of commerce and any location where business people are known to meet and greet. Traditionally, it is said to signify a place where sails for ships and such materials are stored. This would mean shipyards and marinas. Also, together with Libra, lumberyards and places where piles of wood are stacked.

Through Saturn, Capricorn also rules boundaries, thresholds and all structures that divide or restrict rooms and territory. This would reference walls, garden fences, gateposts and even international borders. This would define the property belonging to any individual, such as the boundaries around a home or business. Because it is a winter sign, Capricorn rules all winter elements related to the Earth and the confinement or protection from these elements. This is where it indicates snow sheds, for instance, and bushy places (dens or caves as well) where animals may find cover.

Capricorn is strongly affiliated with government so it often signifies government buildings such as city hall or the chamber of commerce. This rulership is restricted to the actual administration of Government and does not refer to such services as the library or the museums. So it only describes Government offices. It also associates with big business so it may be describing the chamber of commerce or the main business district. Saturn, which rules Capricorn, also implies restrictions so it can bring to mind prisons, cages, traps (low to the ground), dungeons and places where people or animals are trapped and held against their will. This is especially true as it relates to the fur industry, where winter animals (with fur) are caged and held against their will until they are slaughtered for their hide.

Inside the house it is a low dark corner, on or near the floor, doors, closed in or confined spaces, earthy objects and those associated with waste disposal such as trash cans, recycling bins, in sink disposals, chippers and shredders.

Countries & cities: Include Germany (especially Brandenberg, Cleves and Hesse), Albania, Macedonia, Bulgaria, India, the Orkney Isles, Styria in Austria and Oxford in England.

Colours: Principally black or dark brown. Capricorn's influence can add a dark, earthy tone to other colours. As a cold and dry sign it can also indicate colourless, pale, grey or wan shades associated with something that is aged and lacking lustre.

Stones & Metals: Stones and metals fall under the rulership of planets, not signs, but through its association with Saturn, Capricorn has affinity with lead, diamonds, sapphires, lapis lazuli and all ordinary common stones that are not polished.

Direction: South

AQUARIUS

Places: Aquarius, like Capricorn has general rulership over deep wells, quarries, mines and places that are involved in the extraction of minerals from the earth. Under the traditional rulership of Saturn, it also has signification over land that has recently been dug.

As an air sign, Aquarius relates to places that are high off the ground or above the general eye line. Outside it signifies hills, or land that is uneven or with an eccentric skyline. In the 19th century it was given signification over aviation, aeronautic experiments and apparatus that relates that. I still consider it to relate to airplanes, air strips, airports, air traffic controllers and air plane hangers. Anything relating to aeronautical engineering, in fact and even airline companies, individually and as a whole. As the sign of the waterbearer, it is also descriptive of locations near natural or manmade sources of water supply, fountains or springs. This would mostly include smaller bodies of water that remain relatively still and are rather shallow. In the city, this refers mostly to retention ponds and manmade fountains.

Inside the house it signifies the roof, attic rooms, eaves, or places towards the upper part of the house or a specific room. It is traditionally said to signify vineyards 'or places near a little spring or conduit head'. Inside the house this would include taps, showers and may extend to places where all power supplies emerge. Also refers to the electrical lighting system, especially those lights that run overhead such as track lighting. Consider it also describes lighting rods, rooftop power supplies, windmills, and weathervanes, all of which are usually installed on the roof. In the modern world, please also include satellite dishes, wind turbines and security lighting attached to outside eaves.

Countries & cities: Include Russia, Denmark, lower Sweden, modern Central Asia, Northern Iran, Arabia, Croatia, Southern Romania, Westphalia, Hamburg, Bremen and Ingolstadt in Germany, Pesario and Trent in Italy.

Colours: Associated with etherial blue, and sky colours. Sometimes also a muted bluish-ash color.

Stones & Metals: Stones and metals fall under the rulership of planets, not signs, but through its traditional association with Saturn, Aquarius has affinity with lead, diamonds, sapphires, lapis lazuli and all ordinary common stones that are not polished. It also has a particular relationship to marble.

Direction: West by North

PISCES

Places: Pisces is a water sign and is signified by fish so you can assume it refers to fishponds, rivers, springs, watermills, water pumps, wells, marshy or watery ground, moats, springs, the ocean, and all places near to water inside or around the house. Any place where waterfowl, fishes or water plants can be found. This includes beaches, watermills, mossy places (especially near ancient ruins), fisheries, fish canneries, public aquariums, SeaWorld and other amusement parks where people view or play with fish or go swimming. This includes shore excursions on cruises and vacation resorts on the beach. Through it's affiliation with it's ruler, Neptune, and the gravitation towards sacrifice, Pisces also signifies hermitages, monasteries or places of seclusion or retreat. Religious orders and religous rites, most especially those that include sacrifice, either figuratively or in reality.

Inside the house, Pisces points to the bathroom, the sinks, the medicine cabinets (most especially if sleeping medication is also kept there), places where toiletries are stored and cleaning supplies are kept. Pisces rules the feet so it also indicates shoes, shoe boxes, shoe hangers and anywhere else shoes may be kept. All things related to the care of the feet, especially medical in nature. Neptune refers to illegal and legal narcotic drugs so includes places where prescription drugs are kept, especially those that aid sleep or reduce anxiety. Pisces also describes the bathroom and washing area inside the house, especially bath tubs and hot tubs.

In general locations, Pisces rules areas where waterfowl gather, such as seagulls and terns. Also indicates aquariums, shops where aquarium fish are kept and sold, fish mongers, the boats of fishermen, fish canneries and shops that sell fish for food. Can indicate watermills and water plant farms. Also marinas, boatyards, wet storage and small islands that can be reached by boats. Stores and businessees that sell bathing suits, swimming pool accessories, beach balls and suntan lotion, swimming pool and hot tub cleaning equipment, plumbing devices and tools, over the counter medicines (such as pharmacies). Also refers to shoe repair shops, shoe stores, sleep clinics, psychotherapists, massage parlors (especially those with hot tubs), pet groomers (especially for large dogs), dream analysts and fish mongers.

Countries & cities: Include Portugal, Normandy, northern Egypt, Alexandria, Rheims in France, Calabria in Sicily, Worms and Ratisbon in Germany and Compostella in Spain

Colours White and glittering colours.

Stones & Metals: Stones and metals fall under the rulership of planets, not signs, but through its association with Jupiter, Pisces has affinity with crystals, amethysts, clear shining stones (sapphires, emeralds) and marble. Aquamarine, a member of the Beryl family, whose name means 'sea water' seems particularly appropriate to the symbolism of Pisces.

Direction: North by West (northwest)

Houses: Places and Things

Although the only houses that have importance in the forensic chart are the angular houses, there are many times when angular planets are situated in cadent or succeedent houses or have rulership over these houses. Each house in the horoscope describes a different area of our life experience and none can safely be ignored. But those houses with are not angular, do not house angular planets, are not ruled by angular planets and make no aspect to the 4 directions should be ignored in the forensic chart. But herein I will give you the places and things ruled by each and every house none the less, in case an angular planet should reside in one of these areas.

First House / Ascendant

As you already know, the first house is the marker for the subject of the reading. It is an angular house and often in the forensic chart, it describes the victim. You use this house to track the movements of the victim through the rest of the chart. The ruler of this house is a stand in for your subject.

This house also describes that area of the home or local region where the subject spends the most time. It describes objects or belongings that remain in that place closest to the subject. It also describes any people or activities that are occuring around the subject at the time in question.

When the whereabouts of the subject are unknown, this house and it's ruler should give you an idea where he or she is at the time. If the first house ruler is placed in the first house, it shows the subject to be "in his/her place". In general, this means that this subject is in control of their circumstances at the time in question.

This is an angular house and, as such, is swift in motion. It indicates direction east.

Second House

The second house is not an automatic player in the forensic chart. If a planet that rules an angular house lands here, then you must consider it a part of the overall picture. Also, if the ruler of this house disposes of an angular planet or the ruler of the house cusp is sitting an angular house, this applies. Even so, the second house rules the belongings of your subject. This may be her purse, his wallet, her necklace, his gun, her hair brush or his shoes. You get the picture? It can also describe any money the subject had at the time and the role that money plays in the event.

If the second house is found to have power in the chart, then consider the planets that are placed there or the planets that aspect the cusp to determine what the victims' belongings have to do with this event or what role money might play.

The second house is a succeedent house and, as such, is neither swift nor slow in motion. It indicates direction North by East (northeast)

Third House

If a planet in this house is also the ruler of an angular house or disposes of an angular planet, then this house may have power in the event your analyzing. Even so, this house rules the neighborhood the subject is in at the time as well as the neighborhood the subject lives in. It's up to you to decide if this is one and the same. This house also rules vehicles, the front yard of the home, garages and carports in the front of the house. Cars parked in the garage or cars the subject may be riding in or driving. Determine if the subject is in the car by examining the planets in the third house.

This house, more than other, can give direction in the event if angular planets make it a player. If the ruling planet is in this house, it will often mean the subject is being moved, transported in some fashion. The ninth house usually rules larger highways and airplanes while the third is small city streets and ground vehicles like cars and trucks. The ninth house will give large distances, such as international travel, while this house gives local area movement. When you see your subject's ruler in this house you need to examine the chart carefully to determine what direction the vehicle is moving in to see where it might be going. Also note other planets in this house to determine if other people are with him or her at the time.

The third house is a cadent house and, as such, is slow in motion. It indicates direction Northeast.

Fourth House

The fourth house is a power player in the forensic chart and should be considered in your analysis even if there are no planets there. Look to the fourth house ruler for information on the home of the subject, the family members related to the subject, what goes on inside the home of the subject and their current location in general if they are not at their own home. Look at the relation of the seventh house ruler to the fourth house in the chart. This will tell you if the abductor or killer entered the home of the subject, had ever been in the home of the subject and what happened in the home while the intruder was there. You can also use the fourth house ALWAYS as a starting point for timing and direction IF the last place the subject was seen was their home.

The fourth house is an angular house and, as such, is swift in motion. It indicates direction North.

Fifth House

The fifth house has no real power in any given event chart unless the ruler is placed in an angular house, a planet in the fifth disposes of an angular ruler or rules an angular house or the fifth house ruler also rules an angular house or disposes of an angular ruler. As an example, the first house ruler is sitting in the fifth. Under all conditions, the fifth house describes children, the childs bedroom, a playground or groups of kids at schools or nurseries. If the fifth house ruler is also Mercury and the subject is a child, consider Mercury and the fifth house to describe the child. The fifth house also describes romance, sex (reproduction) and physical contact of all kinds (including sports) and combined with angular planets in the eighth house, can describe sex. With the right combinations, this placement can also describe rape and pedophilia. In any case where a child is involved, check this house first.

The fifth house is a succeedent house and, as such, is neither swift nor slow in motion. It indicates direction North by West (northwest)

Sixth House

The sixth house does not have any real power in a forensic chart unless, as always, it has interplay in some manner with an angular planet. In all cases this house describes work, service, physical well being, small pets and the condition of runaways. In cases involving known runaways, the first house ruler or Mercury placed in this house is a clear marker that the child will never be seen again. If angular planets are in this house, check it for the work or service of the subject. In some cases, the seventh house or first house ruler in the sixth house can mean someone in the armed forces, most often the army or the navy. In general, it mostly refers to work and service and if the first house ruler is in the sixth, you can guess that that the subject was at the workplace at the time in question. If the sevent house ruler is in this house, it means that the abductor or attacker was at the workplace during the time in question. This house is key when you are searching for lost or runaway household pets.

The sixth house is a cadent house and, as such, is slow in motion. It indicates direction West by Northwest.

Seventh House

This is an angular house in the event chart and, as such, has great power. It ALWAYS indicates the "other person" in the event, whether this is the abductor, murderer, attacker, co-conspirator or hired gun. In most charts, where the subject is missing, known to be abducted, presumed or known to have been murdered, then this is ALWAYS the perp. Look closely to see when the ruler of this house contacts, through aspect, the ruler of the first. Also watch any and all planets in the seventh house. When you see the first house ruler in this house, you are seeing the subject in contact with "the other person" in this event, whether this is the abductor or someone who helps the child runaway. This house always give you the descriptors of the perp which you can assess by using the house planetary ruler and sign.

The seventh house is an angular house and, as such, is swift in motion. It indicates direction West.

Eighth House

This is one of the "death" houses and is usually a part of the death pattern if one does emerge. It also refers to the finances of the partner (second from the seventh), the financial and sexual motivations of the abductor, the part of death for the victim and other factors, if they apply, such as investments, wills, inheritances, insurance policies and money in the bank. In cases where someone is murdered and the second house is involved, a close look should be taken at the eighth house. It is often the case that a man or woman murders the spouse for insurance money and this is shown in this house. Sexual connotations are also a part of this house position, especially if the fifth house is also highlighted. Often you will find markers in both the eighth and the fifth house combined with violent fixed stars or violent combinations of transiting planets and this type of configuration describes rape or violent sexual assault. This house, although, not an angular house is important to consider in every case where there is violent death or sexual assault.

The eighth house is a succeedent house and, as such, is neither swift nor slow in motion. It indicates direction West by South.

Ninth House

This house describes large areas and long distances and is a marker for international travel or contact with foreigners. Sometimes describes plane flights or crossing borders. Has affinity with importers, smugglers and transporters. Look for large vehicles like buses and trucks. Is a marker for the vehicle of the abductor and the neighborhood he or she lives in (the third house from the seventh). This house will tell you how far the abductor traveled to get to the victim and whether the victim got into the abductors car or went off in their own. Describes the great outdoors and is a great help in locating bodies that have been dumped along highways or in wooded areas. Planets in this house or ruling the cusp of this house can be counted on to describe the abductors vehicle, the color and overall style for instance. There are also athletic or outdoors activities associated with this house and with the fifth house can describe ball fields, play parks and other places young people gather to play games or compete. This house more than any other can tell you if the abductor and the victim remained in the same general area or moved farther away. It will also tell you if the body of the victim was left outdoors, buried or in the open.

The ninth house is a cadent house and, as such, is slow in motion. It indicates direction Southwest.

Tenth House

The tenth house is the highest angular house in the event chart and, as such, has great power. It is on the basic level, the patriarchial figure or the father in the vicims life. It can also describe an older man or a man with great authority if the seventh house is involved. Overall, in general scenes, this is the public place or place of business. If the victims' marker appears in the tenth house, it is often the case that he or she was visiting a store or other place of business. If the victim is a small child and the tenth house ruler aspects Mercury, it is likely that it is describing the father or other male authority figure. In cases where bodies are discovered, the tenth house combined with the ninth house ruler can indicate the presence of the police. In some cases, it will help you figure out what the cops may have overlooked or where they might have made a mistake. The tenth house ruler or planets in the tenth interacting or disposing of planets in the seventh house are describing the business activities of the abductor. These are often prominent in cases where women and children are stolen for business purposes such as black market adoption, child pornography, slave labor or the sex trade. Combinations of tenth house planets with seventh, fifth and eighth house placements are strong indicators of business in photos or film. These combinations are sometimes seen in charts where there has been filming of the actual murder or rape and these films are the business of the murderer. These films are sometimes located for sale on the internet.

The tenth house is an angular house and, as such, is very swift in motion. It indicates direction South.

Eleventh House

The eleventh house has very little power in most event charts and only comes into play when ruling planets reside in the eleventh or aspect the ruler of the eleventh. Most often, this placement indicates friends or associates of the victim and can be helpful in pinning down how he or she met the abductor. Sometimes it is obvious, when the seventh house ruler resides in the eleventh with aspects to the ruler of the first, that the victim knew his or her abductor and may have even considered this person to be a friend. This house also shows associates and peer groups so it must may show the victim at a party in the company of peers but perhaps no close friends. Or it may show the victim at a party, having too much to drink or using drugs (depending on placements of Neptune and fifth house planets) and thus being vulnerable to attack. Overall, the eleventh house is not often a strong player in the event chart, except in those cases where the victim was in the company of friends or peers, whether in danger or not. The most useful information that can be extracted from this house and it's planets is whether the victim's friends were male or female and whether these friends had anything to do with the abduction or murder of the subject in question.

The eleventh house is a succeedent house and, as such, is neither slow nor swift in motion. It indicates direction Southeast by South.

Twelfth House

The twelfth house is one of the "death" houses and is frequently a part of any death pattern that may form. This is the house that ends the circle and so describes the end of life. It is the house of self undoing, seclusion and silence and can also indicate hiding or being in secret. This house can tell you the secrets of the victim, such as they are, and show you where he or she is hiding something that may be important, if indeed they are. It is also the house of confinement and slavery and can indicate the victim is being held against his or her will, especially if Saturn and Pluto are prominent. This is also the house of the end of life in general and can indicate the actual grave. If Saturn is in the twelfth house after a death pattern has formed, consider this placement to indicate the location of the body. If earth signs are involved, the body is buried. If water signs are involved, it was dropped in the water. The twelfth house is very often important in forensic charts because so many victims are taken against their will, put into secret confinement and eventually killed and buried. So watch this house closely if you are dealing with a body locater chart.

The twelfth house is a cadent house and, as such, is slow in motion. It indicates direction East by Southeast.

Planets: Places and Things

In understanding the role that planets play in the forensic chart you have to start with the dignities and qualities of the planets in question. Dignities refer to powerful sign placements of the Sun. Exaltation is the most positive powerful and Fall is the most negative powerful. Detriment is the weakest point any planet can express and also depends upon sign placement.

In the house position of the planets, you have to always remember that a planet has no meaning in the forensic chart unless it is in an angular house and/or aspecting or disposing of an angular planet. Any other placement renders the planet useless in the chart and it should be ignored.

So knowing these things about the placements, please consider the following when taking any planet into account.

THE SUN

Dignities:

Rulership by sign   Leo (by day and night)
Sign of detriment   Aquarius
Place of Exaltation (sign & degree) Aries - 19°
Place of Fall (sign & degree) Libra - 19 °

Triplicity rulership   Fire triplicity by day

Rulership by face (or decanate):

Aries   degrees 11 - 20
Gemini   degrees 21 - 30
Virgo   degrees 1 - 10
Scorpio   degrees 11 - 20
Capricorn degrees 21 - 30

People Signified:

All male royalty, including kings, princes, emperors, dukes, marquesses, earls, barons and monarchs. All political (elected or appointed) officers such as lieutenants, deputy-lieutenants of counties, magistrates, justices of peace, judges, sheriffs, constables, attorney generals, magistrates (of city, town, castle or country village), high ranking bureaucrats and elected officials of all grades and placements. Also describes the men who care for the possessions of royalty such as stewards and caretakers. In general, those men in positions of power for the most part.

Can also describe men who are better than average athletes or hunters, (those activities that gain fame and idolation and require masculine prowess). In everyday occupations, the Sun can refer to goldsmiths, jewelry makers, foundry workers, pewterers, silversmiths, coppersmiths, minters and mints that produce valuable collectibles.

Colours:
Yellow, the colour of gold, scarlet or clear red, some say purple.

Herbs, Plants and Trees:

Any plant or herb that smells pleasantly and have a majestic form. The flowers are most often yellow or red. These flowers would love open areas with lots of sun. Typical plants that associate with the Sun are Saffron, Laurel, Saint Johns Wort, Amber, Musk, Ginger, Balm, Marigold, Rosemary, Cinnamon, Celandine, Eyebright, Peppermint, Rue, Peony, Barley, Arsenic, Cinquefoil and Barley. Some of these plants also associate with other planets so don't get too specific without checking other lists first.

Trees associated with the Sun include the Ash, Palm, Laurel, Walnut, Olive, Bay, Myrrh, Frankincense, Cane, Cedar, Orange and Lemon trees.

Places:

In general, the Sun indicates the houses and courts of royalty, palaces, theatres, all magnificent structures that have a grandoise or elegant form.

Inside the home, it describes halls, dens (with fireplaces) and dining rooms.

Outdoors, beehives and honeycombs associate with the Sun. Also farm areas that grow cereal grains, wild rice, vegetables with a high iron content and fruit that grows on vines.

Miscellaneous:

Yellow or red clothing, gold jewelry, valuable articles, yellow or purple cars or bicycles. Peacocks and Lions. A person who lives in a splendid or upscale, fancy apartment.

Traditional physical descriptions offered:

Usually the Sun represents a man (the Sun is male energy) with a large, strong body. It gives a yellow, sallow complexion, a round, large forehead, go large, sharp and piercing eyes. Blonde or flaxon hair, easily going bald or already bald. If the man has a beard, it will be large and fancy in some manner, well maintained. Ruddy complexion, fleshy body (not necessarily fat but fleshy). Because the personality tends to gravitate to luxury, rich food and fabrics and a life of ease and comfort, there is also a tendency to gain weight and be out of shape. In youth, the body is strong and well formed but a life of ease and pleasure can change that as the man ages.

These men are considered to be generous and magnanimous. Also sincere, positive, big hearted with a high mind. They will not usually stoop to activities they feel are beneath them. In this, a huge ego with good self esteem, values the self. Humane and gentle except when called to battle to defend personal principles or those that he loves.

Remember, however, that these physical descriptions are based on a time in our society when there was little mixture of sex or race and communities were made up of people from similar backgrounds. As a result, the older, traditional readings such as these may not work as well in our current world environment.

THE MOON

Dignities:

Rulership by sign Cancer
Sign of detriment Capricorn
Place of Exaltation (sign & degree) Taurus - 3°
Place of Fall (sign & degree) Scorpio - 3 °
Triplicity rulership Earthly triplicity by night

Rulership by face (or decanate)

Taurus degrees 11 - 20
Cancer degrees 21 - 30
Libra degrees 1 - 10
Sagittarius degrees 11 - 20
Aquarius degrees 21 - 30

People Signified:

All female royalty including queens, countesses, ladies, duchesses, baronesses, empresses and princesses. In fact, all manner of women in general and sometimes also the common folk. The masses, in tandem with Pluto.

In occupations, the Moon describes sailors, fishermen, fishmongers, brewers, tapsters, vintners, letter-carriers, coachmen, huntsmen, messengers, mariners, millers, alewives, malsters, oisterwives, fisherwomen, charwomen, tripewomen, and generally such women as carry commodities in the streets or sell wares on street corners. Food trucks, street vendors and carnival workers. Also refers to midwives, nurses, hackneymen, watermen, waterboys. In modern society, it can describe people who travel long distances for their jobs. This often means musicians, as the Moon has strong affinity with music in general.

In daily life, the Moon can depict wanderers, people who travel for fun and enjoyment, those who like to move around a lot and don't stay in one place for long. Can also describe derelicts, bums, drunks, drug addicts and alcoholics. Has strong affinity with alcohol while Neptune is more closely associated with drugs and drug addiction.

Colors:

White or pale yellowish-white, pale green, or silver. Sometimes a cream color or a spotted cream.

Herbs, Plants and Trees:

Those which have soft and thick juicy leaves, such as succulents. Plants that grow in watery places, such as watercress. Also those plants that grow quickly to a large size. Herbs associated with the Moon include saxifrage, verbena and tarragon.

Fruits ruled by the Moon include yellow and orange melons, watermelons, pineapples, berries, cantaloupes and all fruit with a high water content.

Vegetable plants include white cabbage, red cabbage, turnips, celery, cucumbers, lettuce, broccoli, eggplant and all vegetables with a high water content. Also those plants grown in marshy, dark conditions such as mushrooms and mandrake.

Trees ruled by the moon are those that have round, shady, large spreading leaves and are a little fruitful. In particular, consider the Linden Tree. Consider also trees that produce sap, such as maple.

In areas where flowers may be a part of the scenario, the Moon describes lilies, waterlilies, white roses and white flowers in general. Lilypads, water hyacinth, lotus and any plant that grows in water or floats on water.

Places:

The Moon rules the ocean, fountains, fish ponds, rivers, ponds, common sewers, baths and bath houses. Any and all havens of the sea, including seaside highways and desert or deserted places along shorelines or near waterways, port towns, marinas, riverfronts, canals, oceanfront residences and businesses. Can also describe little bubbling brooks, springs, streams and any body of water where people fish, go boating and play in the water. Can also describe standing pools of water, boggy places, common shorelines, large rivers, small retention ponds, marshes, etc.. Not as dirty as Scorpio and not as foul smelling. Cancer usually signifies watery areas that are frequented by people and somewhat maintained. Scorpio inclines to boggy, nasty areas where hardly anyone goes. Cancer can also refer to that area of the beach where the seaweed has gathered.

In the home, it describes the kitchen and bathroom sinks, the plumbing that connects the sinks, the laundry room, the washer, the dishwasher, the bath tub and the shower. It can describe dishes, dishware, cooking pots and pans, china, silverware and silver or plated items such as serving pieces. Has an affinity with aluminum.

In business, the Moon describes seafood restaurants, beachwear shops, retailers of surfboards, boats, waterskis, swimsuits, etc... Charter boat captains, divers, sunken treasure hunters, silversmiths, jewelry shops, coffeeshops, the vegetable area of the supermarket, vegetable vendors, mines, marinas, boat storage facilities, fish and tackle shops, fishing guides, antique shops, genealogists, the water company.

Miscellenous:

Silver, selenite, all soft stones, crystals. Also has affinity for aluminum, minerals of all kinds and soft, smooth substances.

Traditional Physical descriptions offered:

Usually the Moon describes a woman (feminine in nature) who is generally fair with a white (pale) complexion. She would have a round face, grey or blue eyes, brown hair and full lips. There would much hair both on the head, face, and other parts. This woman may have one eye a little larger than the other; short, plump hands, with the whole body inclining to be fleshy, plump and even obese.

According to traditional readings, If the Moon is afflicted by the Sun in the event chart, the person in question usually has some blemish in, or near the eye.

Overall, the Moon describes a person who is always on the move, never settles down. This person gets involved in many things and many people; can be a busybody. Very talented and clever. The Moon in good aspect with Venus describes a beautiful voice and perhaps someone who sings. This person can also be lazy, involved in frivolous activities and addicted to bad habits. Again, an affinity for alcohol.

Remember, however, that these physical descriptions are based on a time in our society when there was little mixture of sex or race and communities were made up of people from similar backgrounds. As a result, the older, traditional readings such as these may not work as well in our current world environment.

MERCURY

Dignities:

Rulerships by sign   Gemini (by day) / Virgo (by night)
Signs of detriment   Sagittarius & Pisces
Place of Exaltation (sign & degree) Virgo - 15°
Place of Fall (sign & degree) Pisces - 15°

Triplicity rulership: Air triplicity by night

Rulership by face (*or decanate*):

Taurus degrees 1 - 10
Cancer degrees 11 - 20
Virgo degrees 21 - 30
Sagittarius degrees 1 - 10
Aquarius degrees 11 - 20

People Signified:

In general, Mercury describes merchants (and their stores) and messengers, including mail carriers, package delivery persons, emailers, telephone soliciters, bill collectors and the lot. This is a traditional rulership and goes back to the days of war on horseback when armies would wait for hours for messages from the enemy. This is where the term, "don't shoot the messenger" comes from. Can also indicate a theif or a cat burgular, someone who enters the home with the intent of stealing. Someone with fast hands and nimble fingers, such as typists, guitarists, sketchers, cartoonists, gamers, etc. Can indicate an uneducated "lout" with a "loud mouth". Can also signify chatty people like long winded ministers or speakers or the neighbor who is in everyone's business.

In business, it also describes literary folk of all kinds, including writers, publishers, printers, editors, the person who delivers your newspaper and those that leave fliers on your doorstep. Also phonebook publishers and distributors. Mercruy also rules secretaries, scriveners, diviners, sculpturers, poets, orators, advocates and schoolmasters. Because it describes exchangers of money, clerks, accountants and attorneys (the "mouthpeice"), it can signify banks, money converters, investment firms and Wall Street itself. Rules over tailors, seamstresses, clothing makers, pattern designers, sewing machine operators and fabric manufacturers.

In general, Mercury describes philosophers, mathematicians, astrologers, footmen and people who travel on foot.

Colors:

Traditionally, light blue, grey mixed with sky-colour, azure or the color of a dove. Also, mixed and new colors, especially those consisting of many colors mixed in one.

Herbs, Plants and Trees:

Vegetables & nuts ruled by Mercury include beans, filberts, potatoes, kohlrabi, carrots and walnuts. Trees ruled by Mercury include the walnut tree, the elder, oak, chestnut and all trees that bear nuts as fruit. Herbs ruled by Mercury include lungwort, aniseed, marjoram, cardamom, alkanet and caraway. Flowers indicated by Mercury are all brightly colored, small flowers that grow in large numbers. These include buttercups, cat's ear, lily of the valley.

Places:

Merchants and tradesmen's shops, markets, fairs, flea markets, swap meets, car lots and grocery stores. Also rules schools, and shoolyards, groups of children and individual children (including your subject). Common public halls where people meet and linger. Bowling-alleys, tennis courts cars and other vehicles, whether passing by or directly involved, the streets and thoroughfares of the neighborhood and often the neighborhood itself. Storage units, warehouses, paper mills, bookstores, mailboxes, shipping service centers, truckstops, auto repair shops, pawn shops, watch repair, tailors, shoemakers, shoe repair, offices for doctors, optometrists, faxing and printing hubs, accountants, lawyers, managers and professional organizers.

Miscellaneous

Mercury rules quicksilver. Also the milestone, marcasite or fire-stone and all stones or rocks of mixed color. Also rules, generally, all paper money, bills, deeds, books, pictures, scientific merchandise and pens. Also computers, typewriters, autopens and printers.

Traditional Physical Descriptions Offered:

Mercury usually indicates someone who is tall, thin with an upturned nose. Clear complexion with some color in it, but not florid. Brown or hazel eyes with impaired vision, wearing glasses or contacts. This person would have an active, springy walk and would seem to be busy all the time. Talkative, chatty, busybody. Clever, cunning and sometimes scheming with a tendency to steal or at the least take what isn't theirs, even if only for a time. Can be scattered brained and nervous, with an irritable temperment. Impatient and critical.

Remember, however, that these physical descriptions are based on a time in our society when there was little mixture of sex or race and communities were made up of people from similar backgrounds. As a result, the older, traditional readings such as these may not work as well in our current world environment.

<u>VENUS</u>

Dignities:

Rulerships by sign Taurus (by night) / Libra (by day)
Signs of detriment   Aries & Scorpio
Place of Exaltation (sign & degree) Pisces - 27°
Place of Fall (sign & degree) Virgo - 27 °

Triplicity rulership   Earth triplicity by day

People Signified:

Although Venus is a feminine sign, it does not always indicate women. I have seen it indicate the abductor when that person was known to be male. So do not judge it this way. It does, however, indicate many feminine things, such as wives, midwives, mothers, virgins, singers, beauticians, dressmakers and wedding coordinators. But it does not always indicate women. It can often refer to men who do a job most often done by a woman. This might include male hairdressers, fashion designers, chefs, bakers, housecleaners, typists, dancers, etc...

In occupations: Musicians, silkmakers, furriers, linen-drapers, painters, jewellers, lapidaries, embroiderers and women-tailors. Also choir singers, fiddlers, pipers and all people who play music or sing. Also when joined with Moon, really good singers. Also indicates perfumers, artists, engravers, upholsterers, glove and hat makers and everyone who sells those commodities which adorn women either in body (clothes) or in face, (cosmetics.)

In daily life: Players, gamesters, people dancing, singing, rejoicing and having fun. The woman or man who makes dinner, decorates the home or helps fit the dresses or puts on the makeup. The person having the party. The butler, the caterer, the housemaid.

Colors:

The oldest traditions indicate that Venus signifies white, or milky sky-colour mixed with brown, or a little green. Another school of thought attribute Venus to purple or purple-white (bluish). Take your pick.

Herbs, Plants and Trees:

Vegetables and fruit ruled by Venus include apples, figs, olives, oranges, almonds, wheat, peaches, apricots, plums and raisins. Most berries. Trees ruled by Venus include the white rose, white sycamore, wild ash, apple, pear and fig. Herbs ruled by Venus include mugwort, ladies mantle, lemon balm, vervain, millet, valerian, thyme, amber, peppermint, coriander and musk. Flowers ruled by Venus are lily of the valley, maidenhair, violet, daffodils, roses, hydrangea and blue flowers in general.

Places:

In general, Venus indicates gardens, especially those with perfume flowers in pastel and rich colors like roses and pinks. Also, fountains, hotels, lodges, dining rooms, those places where people gather to dance, wheatfields and theatres.

In the home: Venus indicates bridal-chambers, beds, bedrooms, hanging clothing, closets and wardrobes. Also the dining room or entertainment room, especially where music is played and people may dance. Jewelry boxes, lingerie drawers, cosmetic cases and places where makeup is stored. Cabinets where perfume, shampoo and personal care products are kept. Dressing rooms, vanities, mirrors, overstuffed chairs, carpet, wall paper, displayed collectibles and photos of couples. Trinkets. Little girls playhouse or where ever her toys or dolls are kept.

In business: Hotels, theaters, perfume shops, cosmeticians, beauticians, massage parlors, dating services, matchmakers, jewelers, jewelry shops, dancing schools, singing schools, singers, bands, musicians, dancers and dancing companies. Venus also describes theater companies, artists, designers, decorators, wedding coordinators, justice of the peace, remodelers, counselors, talk show hosts, commentators, broadcasters and style advisors.

Miscellaneous:

Venus rules copper, brass and bronze. Stones include the cornelian, the sky-coloured sapphire, white and red coral, marcasite, alabaster, lapis lazuli, beryl and chrysolite. Also rings, costume jewelry, perfume bottles, makeup cases and wine bottles. Also rules the dove, cat, rabbit and swan.

Traditional Physical Descriptions Offered:

Venus traditionally rules women and womanly things. However, it often describes a male with beautiful or feminine qualities. Venus is associated with dimples and fair, curly hair. It often describes beauty. The person indicated by Venus will be attractive and physically soft and shapely. Males described by Venus would have sculpted muscles that look fleshy and soft even if they aren't. Both males and females will have noticeable hips. This person can also be corpulent (fat) because the are self indulgent and often lazy. The love of good food (associated with Taurus) and a life of ease and luxury (associated with Libra) can make the native a "lounger" who does not like to work. Look for a cleft chin, dimples in the cheeks, fair colored (often curly) hair and "dove" eyes that can be either blue or brown. This person would also have a lovely voice and could be a talented singer.

Remember, however, that these physical descriptions are based on a time in our society when there was little mixture of sex or race and communities were made up of people from similar backgrounds. As a result, the older, traditional readings such as these may not work as well in our current world environment.

MARS

Dignities:

Rulerships by sign Aries (by day) / Scorpio (by night)
Signs of detriment Libra & Taurus
Place of Exaltation (sign & degree) Capricorn - 28°
Place of Fall (sign & degree) Cancer - 28 °

Triplicity rulership Water triplicity by day & night

People Signified:

Although Mars is a masculine sign, it does not always indicate men. I have seen it indicate the victim when that person was known to be female. So do not judge it this way. It does, however, indicate many masculine things, such as generals of armys, colonels, captains, as well as tyrants, usurpers, new conquerors or Princes ruling by tyranny or oppression. But it does not always indicate men. As I will show you it has qualities that apply to women as well to men. And many women are involved in occupations traditionally defined by Mars.

In occupations: surgeons and physicians, butchers, marshals and all those who use weapons in their work or work with weapons such as gunners, gun toolers, gunsmiths and cutlers of swords and knives. This includes people who use weapons to enforce the law such as marshals, sergeants, police officers, bailiffs, bounty hunters and executioners. Other occupations that use sharp or weaponlike instruments include barbers, tailors, carpenters, cooks, watch makers and taxidermists. Include under the rulership of Mars those that work with heat as well, such as bakers, dyers, chefs, tanners, blacksmiths, foundry workers and apothecaries.

In daily life: Mars can indicate outlaws, renegades and theives. Also people with authority that is strongly enforced, such as disciplinarians or parents with strict rules and punishments. In the family, it describes the father or father figure. Also describes athletes, competitors, ambitious business persons, CEOs and Presidents. People who take aggressive action or attack others; can describe violence and intimidation. People who work or play with fire, including arsenists or people who like to smoke their food.

Colors:

The oldest traditions indicate that Mars signifies red, yellow, fiery and shining. I consider it to mostly describe a fiery red or scarlet color and not so much the yellow, which I attribute to Leo or the Sun.

Herbs, Plants and Trees:

Be sure that this includes hose that are red in colour, whose leaves are pointed and sharp, whose taste is caustic and burning, that love to grow in dry places, are corrosive and penetrate the flesh and bones with a subtle heat! This is the traditional reading and I cannot argue with it. I consider Mars to signifty the nettle, first and foremost, and also spurge, onions, garlic, mustard, ginger, leeks, horehound, hemlock, tamarind and prickly pear cactus. Also I think it describes thistle, which is brambly and prickly. Actually all brambly plants must be considered so when looking at an area that is sandy, dry, hot and full of brambly, prickly plants, consider Mars as a marker.

Mars also describes devils milk, radish, chili peppers, cayenne, jalapenos and other hot peppers, peppermint, capers, hops, shallots, fir trees and all trees with thorns or thorny nuts like chestnuts.

Places:

In general, Mars indicates war machinery, war memorials, statues of bronze, iron and steel; minerals in general and all steel and iron mines. Sparkling and fiery substances.

In the home: Mars indicates chimneys, furnaces, fireplaces, grills and forges. Red wines, red garments, red accessories such as purses, hats and shoes. Brass collectibles, iron statues in the home or garden, jewelry with fiery gemstones like rubies or opals. Sharp instruments used in the home such as scissors, kitchen knives, razors, shavers, power saws and pocket knives. Abrasive instruments used in the home such as sanders, lint shavers, fingernail files and paint scrapers.

In business: Blacksmiths and other smiting or smithing operations, including coin smelting and horseshoe smithing. Shops that use or sell furnaces, fireplaces or fireplace supplies. Slaughterhouses, butcher shops, bakeries and any business where knives or fire are used. Also places where bricks or charcoal is burnt, such as public grills, barbecues, smokehouses and restaurants with open pits.

Miscellaneous:

Mars rules iron and steel. Also rules the eagle, tiger, wolf and scorpion.

Traditional Physical Descriptions Offered:

Mars traditionally rules men and manly things. However, it often describes a female with strong and masculine qualities. Mars is associated with a strong physique, muscular form and athletic prowess. It also describes strength and ambition. The person indicated by Mars will be strong willed and strong in the body with an athletic, well formed physique. This will be a "hard body" that is obviously active and "in shape". There will be hard cuts to the muscle physique and both men and women will have the look of a well toned athlete. But remember that athletes can also be gymnasts, dancers, surfers and bicyclists, all forms of exercise favored by women. This person will never be fat or out of shape. They are not lazy. They like to get things done, have ambition to the be the "first" and the "best" and won't put up with diddling around. Other than the great physique, look for a strong chin and a broad forehead. Traditional readings give a longer, oval face with high set ears that stand out. A "military" look would be one way of describing it. These people are "uniform" even when they aren't in uniform and they do tend to be in the military. This is especially true if Mars rules the first and is placed in the sixth. Look also for a longish nose and a reddish tint to the hair.

Remember, however, that these physical descriptions are based on a time in our society when there was little mixture of sex or race and communities were made up of people from similar backgrounds. As a result, the older, traditional readings such as these may not work as well in our current world environment.

JUPITER

Dignities:

Rulerships by sign Sagittarius (by day) / Pisces (by night)
Signs of detriment Gemini & Virgo
Place of Exaltation Cancer - 15°
Place of Fall Capricorn - 15 °

Triplicity rulership   Fire triplicity by night

People Signified:

Jupiter is an expansive planet that describes people and places that are large in some manner. But it is also benevolent and positive in energy so most of these places and people are of a benign or well meaning character. It rules higher education (colleges and universities), the profession of law (law libraries and universities), the profession of religion (churches and church leaders) and the healing places (hospitals and surgical centers). Because of it's expansive largesse, Jupiter also rules thickness and richness in anything. Such would be wool fabrics (thick and rich), rich foods, large, ornate presentations of any kind, from fancy churches with stained glass and gold to government buildings with ornate finishings, such as that commonly found on large courthouses and city centers.

In occupations: Any occupation that holds a vast expanse of power and the ability to bestow generosity on others. This would include judges, bishops, priests, ministers, cardinals, chancellors (all who have the power to forgive, to send you to jail for life or damn you to hell). Also senators and councillors, lawyers, doctors of civil law and counselors. In general, clothiers, drapers, and upholsterers (those who use heavy fabrics in large amounts). Also people who work with tin, miners (mineral mines), horse trainers and orchard farmers.

 In daily life: In general, all ecclesiastical men, including priests and altar boys. Also young scholars and students in a university or college, professors, teachers and the school itself (especially grand universities with lots of land and ornate buildings).

Colors:

The oldest traditions indicate that Jupiter signifies sea-green or blue or purple (red mixed with green or blue). Also an ash color, a mixed yellow and green.

Herbs, Plants and Trees:

Jupiter describes large trees that are both tall and thick. Any tree that is huge in size and intimidating. This includes large, old oak trees with sprawling roots, the giant sequoia, the California redwood, Oregon pines, douglas firs and spruce trees and other trees that are tall, bushy and sprawling. Also included are some types of eucalyptus, mountain ash, Tasmanian blue gum trees and centenary trees, among others. In general, Jupiter also describes cherry trees, birches, mulberries, barberry trees, olive trees, and almond trees.

Among spices, Jupiter rules cloves, clove sugar mixes, mace, nutmeg, wild oregano, sage, liquorice, mint, saffron and mace. Among herbs, Jupiter rules the gilly flower, balsam, flax, lungwort, selfheal, borage, bugloss, willow, liverwort and milk thistle (both of which treat the liver, which Jupiter rules). Among fruits, Jupiter rules strawberries, figs, dried grapes (raisins), rhubarb, pears, gooseberries, milberries and mulberries. Among flowers, Jupiter rules violets, peonies, daisies, carnations, dandelions and pimpernels.

Jupiter also rules ivy (all forms of ivy) and wheat (including wheatfields) which Virgo also rules.

Places:

In general, Jupiter describes churches and their alters. This includes places where churchmen and women gather, such as synods and convocations. Also describes wardrobes of all kinds, whether public or private, in shops or in the home. Courts of justice and all offices and buildings associated with justice, such as courtrooms and courthouses. Also public oratories, where speeches are given such as convention halls, presentation rooms, meeting halls, etc..; those places where people gather to hear people speak with authority. Also Jupiter is noted to represent all "curious" places that are unfamiliar and intriguing, especially if the place is "neat" and not in disarray. I know this seems strange but this is a traditional reading and it has been proven in horary.

In the home: Jupiter indicates wardrobes, whether in closets or not and especially those areas where coats and wool clothing are stored. That area of the closet given to the man's clothing and belongings, especially upscale items and tailored jackets. Horse stables, horses and the tack and hay that is stored nearby. Also rules domestic fowls such as backyard chickens or any caged birds to be used for food. Jupiter also describes the private garage attached to the home. Especially the larger ones with doors. Metal goods within the home such as cooking tins, metal flatware, steel doors or ladders, etc.. Jupiter can also indicate the woods behind the home if that wooded area is vast. Also an orchard, if there is one and it is substantial. Consider also any area in the home for religious observance, whether a private alter, a display of bibles or prayer books or pictures of deities.

In business: Jupiter represents the church and thereby also priests, preachers, nuns, bishops, cardinals, chaplains, etc.. anyone who speaks or preaches a religion, whether Christian or not. Also courts of justice, so lawyers offices, judges chambers, justice of the peace, clerks of the court and probate (that is also assigned to the eighth house). With affinity for wardrobes, Jupiter describes tailors of men's clothing, designers and manufacturers of wool articles, coat and jacket stores and haberdasheries. With affinity for orchards, Jupiter also describes winemakers, wineries, merchants who sell and distribute wine. Also horse trainers, ranches with horseback riding, dressage trainers and horse racers, racing emporiums and everyone who profits from horses.

Miscellaneous:

Jupiter designates any large expanse of land, wooded areas, orchards, large bushes. Tailored clothing for men, especially woolen items; horses (through sagittarius) and stables where they are kept. With Mars, it indicates horse slaughterhouses. Also private garages, large mailbox depots, expansive parking lots (such as at airports) and large open areas with rich resources.

Jupiter also rules, in general: honey, oil, most fruits, the elephant and the whale.

Traditional Physical Descriptions Offered:

Jupiter usually describes a large person, either large in size through height and frame or also corpulent. Jupiter rising, for instance, can give a woman a very large head and face or a man a very tall, large stature. Think LBJ. He was a Virgo with Jupiter rising. So this person is probably tall, to start with. Also, this person would stand upright and have a strong carriage. Traditionally, Jupiter gives an oval face with wide open eyes. The eyes are usually hazel gray or a dark brown. Gives a long, wide shaped nose with large nostrils. Also a well shaped mouth with a firm chin. The men would have full heads of dark hair in youth and tend to get bald with age.

Altogether, Jupiter gives a strong, impressive countenance. I usually think of hammy hands and big feet when I think of Jupiter. This a friendly, outgoing, self promoting individual that always has the hand out to shake yours. This person is a politician by nature and personality. Generous with time and energy, always willing to get involved, this person is often the "go to" person of the neighborhood. As a result, this person gets promoted to positions, such as head of the condo association or the community watch group and then, from there, to city council and onward and upward.

Remember, however, that these physical descriptions are based on a time in our society when there was little mixture of sex or race and communities were made up of people from similar backgrounds. As a result, the older, traditional readings such as these may not work as well in our current world environment.

SATURN

Dignities:

Rulerships by sign Capricorn (by night) / Aquarius (by day)
Signs of detriment Cancer & Leo
Place of Exaltation Libra - 21°
Place of Fall Aries - 21 °

Triplicity rulership Air triplicity by day

People Signified:

In general Saturn signifies people who own land or farm the land. It also describes the poor and needy, beggars, day laborers, slaves and prisoners. Because Saturn relates to old age, it refers to fathers, grandfathers, genealogists and family historians. In general, a dead person or a person who has been buried; the dead body; the bones of the dead body.

In occupations: Saturn describes curriers, herdsmen, shepards and ranchers. Also night farmers, miners under ground, potters, brick makers and ditch diggers. Any occupation that works with tin. Also broom makers, chimney sweepers and chandlers. Because of it's association with underground activity, Saturn can be describing a plumber. Also morticians, who bury people under ground. And gardeners, because they plant things underground.

In daily life: Saturn can describe clowns (at the circus or the birthday party). Also pall bearers at the funeral. Everyone who scavenges and collects, including dumpster divers and garbage sifters. In religions, Saturn can imply Jesuits or Sectarists. Also, monks (in seclusion). Anyone who is strong on discipline and harsh in character, not afraid of sacrifice and hard work.

Colors:

Traditionally, Saturn describes dark, sad, ashy colours, black. I have found it to also signify a dark, drab green such as olive or army green.

Herbs, Plants and Trees:

Among trees, Saturn rules scraggly, old, thinly leaved trees that are scarred. Tamarisk is a good example, with it's scalelike leaves and very thin twigs; it grows in arid, barren deserts. Also the thin, sparse savine trees and senna. Also rules the willow (or sallow) tree, yews, cyrpess, hem and pine trees.

Among spices, Saturn describes poppy seeds, sage and cumin. Among herbs, Saturn descrbies bearsfoot, wolf bane, hemlock, hellebore, burdock, vervain, mandrake, poppy and poppy seeds, rue, nightshade, angelica, box elder, orache (or golden herb), shepards purse and horsetail. Among vegetables, Saturn describes parsnip, spinach, capers, hemp, barley and bran. Among flowers, Saturn describes poppies, pansies, cornflowers, knapweed and any flower that can grow under barren, dry or distressed conditions. Saturn does not signify any fruit.

Places:

In general, Saturn describes deserts, gravel areas, places with sand and no plant life except weeds. Also, it describes woods, mostly dark wooded areas that are inaccessible and hard to navigate. Saturn also includes obscure valleys, caves, dens and deep, dark holes in the ground. Favors really sandy, dusty areas. All ruinous, run down and abandoned buildings. Any dirty, stinking, muddy place that is inaccessible and hard to navigate. Any place where people have been buried or where a buried body may be found. Also, mountains especially if they are craggy, rocky and inaccessible.

In the home: Sinks, wells, underground storage for water or earth. Compost heaps. Underground plumbing. Cellars, basements and attics. Places that are dirty, old, dusty and dark. Dark colored wool or heavy garments hung in a dark part of the closet. Agricultural implements, including the lawn mower, the hoe, the shovel, the clippers, weed eaters and anything else used in the home to turn up the earth for gardening. Deep water wells. Wooden furniture, especially those old, battered items that are held together with glue. Also rules glue, tape and rope, anything that binds. The gravel driveway. Also, leather goods such as the couch or the jacket in the closet. Sandy areas around the outside of the home, those places with nothing but dirt and weeds and possibly also gravel.

In business: Saturn rules cemetaries, grave yards, church-yards, morticians and grave diggers. Also, any business that operates underground, such as coal mines, plumbers, foundation layers. Also wood working occupations such as carpenter, whittler or furniture maker. Shops that sell antiques, especially fine antique wood furniture. Also tinsmiths (people who make tin cans) and people who work with lead (such as pencil makers) or artists that use pencils. Tanners and leathermakers. Cattlemen who sell cow skins for leather and tanning. Taxidermists who immortalize dead animals. Graveyards with headstones that immortalize dead humans.

Miscellaneous:

Saturn often describes lead, the lead-stone, the dross of all metals, also the dust and rubbidge of every thing. Garbage dumps and landfills. Saturn rules stones like sapphire, lapis lazuli, onyx and all black, ugly country stones not polishable, and of a sad ashy or black colour. Also gravel, gravel full of gray stones, rubble. Saturn can also describe ferns, especially finger ferns and holly. Rules the mule and the donkey.

Traditional Physical Descriptions Offered:

Saturn usually describes an older person and perhaps one who is very old, wrinkled and graying. Also describes people of all appearances who are very poor, living a hard life, hard scrabble, struggling. Saturn is the planet of sacrifice and challenge, creating hardships for many. In descriptors, it will give you a person who is having a tough time. Traditional descriptors have a bony, thin person with a dull, sallow complexion. This would also be a strong person, though, unless very old and weakened by age. The younger person signified by Saturn has a strong stride, gives an air of self control and discipline. This person believes in hard work and expects this from others; does not shy from drudgery the way most people do. Traditional readings give black or dark brown, thinning, straight hair with dark blue or brown eyes that are sharp and peircing. There would be a thin face, thin fingers and a bony overall appearance. These people do not take joy in eating or indulging themselves. This person would work hard and save every penny and not have a home full of toys and personal items. Just the necessities. Not much of a talker. Cold and distant; strange tastes; finds enjoyment in "different" activities than most. Dry sense of humor.

Remember, however, that these physical descriptions are based on a time in our society when there was little mixture of sex or race and communities were made up of people from similar backgrounds. As a result, the older, traditional readings such as these may not work as well in our current world environment.

URANUS

Descriptors Associated with Uranus:

Aloof; altruistic; cool; critical; crushingly assertive; conscious of personal authority and power; directed by inner impulses; eccentric; erratic; firmly opinioned; obstinate, frequently fatalistic regarding personal destiny; heroic; iconoclastic; illuminating; imaginative; impersonal; impulsive; ingenious; independence; innovation; new ideas, new methods, new moral codes; liberating;

moved by new circumstances; off-hand; organising; peculiar; positive; persevering; power-conscious; promoting; prone to sudden changes of mind and view; prophetic; revolutionary; romantic; self-centred; self-reliant; spasmodic; spontaneous; unbendingly wilful; unsentimental; variable; and violently reactive against potential restrictions of freedom of thought and action; but when restricted, potentially anarchistic; bohemian; eccentric; fanatical; and invective and sarcastic without provocation.

People Signified:

In general Uranus signifies people who exhibit contempt for conventional conceptions of morality and a distaste at being controlled. These people dislike arbitrary forms of outside authority. They have executive ability, often flashes of intuition, a natural and reliable insight into others' personal motivations and, in general, an interest in the principles of religion and science and in scientific investigation of material phenomena. These people have an inclination to part with customs but they also have a mechanical ability that favors engineering. These types can include antiquarians, astrologers, discoverers, inventors, lecturers, mesmerists, metaphysicians, original thinkers, patentees, pioneers, travellers and all others who have interest in unique or uncanny things.

In occupations: Uranus describes aviators, engineers, elected government or civic officials, electrical and scientific goods traders, electricians, civic officials, phrenologists, psychologists, public functionaries, radio technicians, spirit mediums and all pursuing uncommon forms of work.

 Any occupation that has the ability or propensity to smash and transform outdated & established Saturnian structures and restrictions. Uranus signifies everything anomalous or unconventional. So this could mean anarchists, terrorists, bombers and activists. It can also describe progressives, geniuses, scientific researchers, transformational gurus and religious leaders, as well as inventors of technology that changes the world.

In daily life: Uranus can describe bereavements, blind impulses, catastrophes, changes (especially sudden changes), constructive and mechanical abilities in children or unexpected people. It can also describe for us our enemies and estrangements. Often it refers to exiles and people rejected by the rest of society. In converse, it can describe people in power or authority, public affairs and government. In personal events, it often predicts romances, sudden events, sorrows, suicides, tragedies, and uncertain fortunes.

Colors:

Traditionally, Uranus describes mingled colors and often those that are mixed to create new colors. It also refers to plaids, checks and mixed designs. Color patterns that confuse the eye. Associates with bright or electric blue. Turquoise.

Herbs, Plants and Trees:

Among trees, Uranus rules stark, dramatic trees that are unusually large or small. Also rules trees with fruit that is dangerous or forbidden. Fruit trees associated with Aquarius as well, including fruits that are poison or inedible. Among spices, Uranus describes any spice with a sharp, unusual flavor such as chilis, chili pepper, black or white pepper, cloves or garlic. Among herbs, Uranus rules clove, mistletoe, foxglove, rosemary, and valerian. Among vegetables, Uranus describes collards, turnips, horseradish and any vegetable with a sharp, tangy flavor.

Among flowers, Uranus describes elderflowers, orchids, himalayan poppies (blue), hydrangea (Nikko Blue) and any flower that is a true blue, including blue variants of other flowers. Among fruits, Uranus rules many different kinds. It rules the pear, the starfruit, kiwi fruit, limes and lemons, kumquats, blueberries, eggplant and any fruit which is naturally blue.

Places:

In general, Uranus describes railways, steam engines, gas tanks, asylumns, infirmaries, railway stations, workhouses, airports, places of confinement (including prisons), areas where the ground has been turned, such as in new construction or in preparing soil, the sky, work camps, terrorist hideouts, clubhouses, meeting places for anarchists and revolutionaries, the internet, think tanks.

In the home: the attic, places where antiques are stored, fireplace mantels, outer walls, radios, televisions, ham radios, coin collections, the microwave, any part of the home added on after it was built. Any area of the yard or garden that has been dug up or where the soil has been turned. Arbor or area with tall trees or grove with fruit trees. Lightening rods, satellite dishes and radio antennae. Media rooms, meeting rooms, hidden passageways and unfinished parts of the building or land.

In business: Uranus rules railroads, greyhound bus stations, airports and airways, uranium and radium mines, electricians shops, TV repair shops, businesses that use heavy machinery. Power plants, gas stations, engineering offices, pawn shops, internet businesses, auction houses, strip mining companies, weatherstations, helioports, emergency rooms, infirmaries (in prisons), prison, slave camps, businesses involved in the attempt to overthrow the government. Any business that relies on invention and constant change. Telecommunications, computers, the internet and any effort involving engineering and invention.

Miscellaneous:

Physically, Uranus governs the appendix; aura; brain and stomach membranes; breathing; electromagnetic forces; eyes; heart valves; motor nerves; nerve fluids; and the growth of long bones. When prominent, it confers a pleasing though ascetic or effeminate appearance; slim body; large, light, brilliant, keen eyes; and irregular features.

NEPTUNE

Descriptors Associated with Neptune:

Aesthetic; amorphous; attuned to beauty (and it's imperfections), and attuned also to feeling and mind. Can be described as blissful, compassionate, diffuse and at times subjective, unclear and/or confused. Neptune is also known to be dreamy, ethereal, highly emotional and often times enthusiastic. There are strong talents that make Neptune imitative, impressionable (especially through extra-sensory channels), intuitive and mystical. Combined with a mystery-loving nature, there is an inclination to seek answers and to be investigative. They are spiritually sensitive and are either very religious or involved in a metaphysical pursuit and make great mediums, psychics and prophets.

Neptune is also peaceful, romantic, compassionate and highly sympathetic. There is a silent subtlety but creates a kind of instability that causes the individual to renege on promises.

They can be highly self deceptive and dishonest to all. Neptune does incline to the fine arts and therefor gives talent and interest in dancc, poetry, rhythmn, stringed instruments (in particular such as the harp) and a love of symmetry.

Neptune in charts signifies ambushes, covert alliances, deceptions, schemes or ventures unrevealed and even disguises and ruses. Where ever Neptune appears there is chaos, desire, emotion, erotic energy, illusion and delusion. Can imply imposters, dreamers, false hope, frauds, over imagination and intrigues. There is a susceptibility to drugs and self delusion, intangible emotions, morbidity and suicide as well as sudden death.

People Signified:

In general Neptune signifies those engaged in aesthetic, artistic, inspirational, literary, occult and psychic vocations (including mediums and mystics), or those connected with water. This includes artists, poets, mimes, movie and music collectors and enthusiasts, liars, illusionists, magicians, theives, mediums, prophets, religious cult leaders, religious zealots, aquariums, fish, fishermen, drug abusers, alcoholics, drug pushers, smugglers, submariners, navy personnel, scuba divers and spirit channelers.

In occupations: Neptune describes musicians, photographers, painters, dancers, movie producers, filmographers, photogs, fisheries, fishermen, fish mongers, deep sea divers, fish canneries, pharmacies, pharmaceutical companies, sailors, midshipmen, ship builders, oceanographers, oil companies, oil drilling operations, deep sea oil drilling operations, underwater photographers and film makers. Also, because of the association with compassion and charity, Neptune also describes nurses and caretakers and hospitals, where people are treated for illness and pain. It also rules over pain medication and opiates and the dependancies these drugs create. Rehab centers, physical therapists, counselors, psychotherapists. Sleep therapists, sleep clinics and places where people sleep.

In daily life: Neptune describes preists, preachers, advisors, gurus and support groups. It represents prayer and the faith in a higher power. Neptune describes sailors or people who enjoy water sports. It also describes pot smoking kids who won't get jobs. Someone who was greatly loved yet committed suicide. The fantasy lover. The crush. Neptune is also the local charity, the food bank and the church; in particular the people who serve there. It rules political campaigns and the politicians who run them. The person who cleans the swimming pool or maintains the aquarium. Neptune is also the woman or man the spouse is cheating with; the gigolo or gold digger who pursues and chases. Neptune is also the mystic, the person who predicts your future or the medium that contacts dead relatives. Especially so if these people are doing this work for free. This is the saint or the sinner, the giver or the taker, the liar or the ultimate truth. These people are obviously devoted but they can certainly be unreliable.

Colors:

Traditionally, Neptune describes white, pearlized shades with changing colors (such as you find in a opal or a mother of pearl). Sheer, transformative colors that appear to one color in one view and another in a different view. Any color that is near to transparent. Pure, glistening white. The gemstone most closely associated with Neptune is the colorless Moonstone.

Herbs, Plants and Trees:

Among trees, Neptune rules haggard trees with lots of branches that are thick with foilage and dark. Long branches without foilage, brambling and twisted. The willow tree is a perfect example. Any tree growing along a large waterway. Among spices, Neptune rules sugar, lime flowers, pumpkin and melon seeds. Among herbs, Neptune is most closely associated with Chicory but can also indicate mosses or mosslike herbs.

Places:

In general, Neptune describes deep water and waterways, which includes the ocean, large rivers, deep ponds and lakes. Places where people fish and swim. Also any place where illusions play a large part of the scenario such as funhouses and magic shows. Also any place involved in the recreation of reality, such as a movie theater or stage. Also places where drugs are taken, alcohol is used and people pretend. This includes nightclubs, drug houses, dating mills, houses of prostitution, performance studios (with hairdressers and makeup artists). Costume parties. Any secret and mysterious place that has not been explored. Deep caves, especially those that are underwater. Old mines and deep water wells.

In the home: The bathroom, closet, hiding place or storage place that is dark and quiet. Basements, especially where the plumbing is exposed and / or water on the floor or condensation on the walls. Those places where photos and momentos are displayed. Swimming pools, lakes or ponds on the property, but usually those that are unusually deep and naturally created by rain or runoff. Nearby bodies of water, such as the ocean, a river or a stream. Those bodies of water that have fish such as a Koi pond or fish reserve on the property. Washrooms, medicine cabinets, sick rooms. Through affiliation with Pisces, which rules the feet, Neptune indicates shoes, shoe closets or boxes, those places where shoes are kept in the home. Also, aquariums and fish tanks.

In business: Neptune describes meditation, dreaming, imagination and fantasy. It describes charities, charitable people, bums, those dependant on charity, also bogus companies, theives and liars. Scam artists, pirates and con men. Mostly illegitimate business but for those that are legitimate, they would include photographers, photo studios, beauticians, artists, decoraters, matchmakers, dance studios, mediums, psychics, sleep clinics, pharmacies, scuba classes, deep sea divers, treasure hunters, mining operations, deep sea oil rigs, oil companies, fishermen, scallop and shrimp boats, crabbers, fishmongers. All those occupations listed above as well.

Miscellaneous:

Physically, Neptune governs the cerebral ventricles and pineal gland. It is involved in cell development and reproduction. Rules the glands (the pineal gland and adrenal glands especially). Rules the optic nerves, respiratory and throat issues, the spinal fluid, the tears and the white corpuscules. It can indicate poisoning or drug overdose as cause of death.

In describing the physical nature, it confers a slim, orderly body. Large, hypnotic eyes with a mysterious expression. Sometimes describes sharp, almost cruel features with thin lips. Traditionally it gives a long head, bald at the temples.

PLUTO

Descriptors Associated with Pluto:

Dark, mysterious, ever changing, chaotic, volcanic, passionate, destructive. Can be described as anarchist, violent, evolving, growing, expanding and explosive. Pluto is also known to be sexual, volatile, disruptive, awakening and the cause of ephiphany. There are strong talents that make Pluto creative, inventive, brave, dynamic, desirous of change, revolutionary, fomenting, forceful and challenging. Combined with a creative and adventurous nature, there is an inclination to be inventive and forward thinking. Plutonians are passionate, spiritually charged, heroic and unfraid of circumstances that would have anyone else quaking in their shoes.

Pluto is also revealing, eye opening, shocking and outrageous, bringing in the new by sweeping away the old. There is an overt anarchy that creates a kind of instability that causes the individual to change on a moments notice. They can be very aggressive and demanding, scaring off more sensitive personalities. Pluto does incline to the the business of change and it's influence is found in recycling businesses and garbage companies where things are swept away and hidden or they are changed into something new. Pluto also holds sway over war and the change the world undergoes during times of war. It rules weapons and the instruments of death. Pluto also rules the underworld and the activities of those who live outside the law. It rules mobsters, drug dealers, agents of war, spies, treasoners, murderers, the act of murder, violence in all forms and natural disasters.

Pluto in charts signifies change in the course of events by outside forces or violence.

People Signified:

In general Pluto signifies those engaged in discovery, investigation, subterfuge, criminal activity, research, anarchy, reclamation or those dedicated to change. This includes activists, investigators, researchers, developers, contractors, self improvement gurus and buffs, remodelers, storm trackers, meteorologists, seismologists, heroes, first responders, people who prepare others for disaster, soldiers, warriors, advocates and anyone dedicated to change.

In occupations: Pluto signifes recyclers, garbage collectors, disaster mitigation crews, first responders, political activists, criminals, mobsters, agents of war, spies, seismologists, storm trackers, geologists, anthropologists, funeral directors, hangmen, firebrand preachers and churches dedicated to unusual and disruptive beliefs. Also, because of the association with subconcious forces, Pluto can sometimes indicate psychotherapists, psychiatrists, physical therapists, oncologists, drug pushers, hypnotists, radiologists, social reformers and gurus who advocate for radical change . It also rules over the underworld and anything under the ground, especially those things related to disposal such as plumbing, sewer pipes, cesspools, trash dumps, landfills and retention ponds. It is a marker for sinkholes, volcanoes, tornados and any area of the ground or water that is unstable and unsafe.

In daily life: Pluto refers to those people who enter your life and change it drastically. It also refers to the sudden visit from a stranger. Day to day people include remodelers, rennovators, developers or anyone who changes the environment. It also describes anarchists and rebels who just don't fit in and won't play by the rules. Someone who is safe and secure but yearns for a risky lifestyle. The passionate lover. The challenger and upsetter; the man or woman who hypnotises you and causes you to cheat on your partner. Pluto is also the local political movement and challenger to the status quo. It can describe political campaigns and the politicians who run them, especially those from third parties or from fringe groups. The person who fixes your plumbing and runs the pipes underground. Pluto is also the woman or man that causes you to leave your spouse. Pluto is also the violent aggressor, the stalker, the person who won't take no for an answer. This is the game changer, the person or event that enters your life and changes it forever, for better or for worse. It can mean violent death at the hands of a violent person. Pluto obviously dangerous but it can certainly be exciting as well.

Colors:

Traditionally, Pluto describes black, the kind of dead black that is chalky and thick and opaque. Utter darkness and no light.

Herbs, Plants and Trees:

Among trees, Pluto rules those that are growing in impossible conditions. Any tree growing in a desert, on a rock, in a swamp or in rocky sand. The dramatic tree that seems to stand out among the others. The tree that doesn't belong. Can also indicate trees with thorns and those with no leaves. Among spices, Pluto rules sharp or strong flavors such as catmint, peppermint, witch hazel and hawthorn berries. Among vegetables, Pluto rules pickles and onions. Among herbs and flowers, Pluto is most closely associated with honeysuckle, geranium and rhodedendron.

Places:

In general, Pluto describes dark, mysterious and musty places like caves and basements. Places that are dangerous like waterfalls, whirlpools, craggy mountainsides, swamps, thorny patches, rocky deserts and places swarming with stinging insects. Also any place where change plays a large part of the landscape such as construction sites or places that are under rennovation. Also any place involved in the destruction of the status quo, such as political ralleys or sites attacked by terrorists or anarchists. The site of 911 is a perfect example of a place that was destroyed by terrorists and then rennovated into something amazing. Pluto also rules places where criminal activity is conducted such as illegal gambling parlors, businesses that laundry money, mobster owned casinos and nightclubs. Also, dangerous and dark place that has not been explored. Caves, bunkers, basements and places where things are hidden, especially those that are under ground.

In the home: Unfinished areas of the home. Areas that are under renovation or demolition. Junk piles, garbage cans, sewers, toilets, septic tanks, sludge and runoff, dirty, clogged gutters and soffits and eaves that are infested with pests or clogged with debris. Attics or basements if they are dark, dirty, water logged or damp and moldy. On the property, any area rotted away by water or debris, such as sinking ground, walls that are crumbling, roofs that are caving in from rot or mold. Pluto does not indicate barren ground but land that his blighted is his dominion, including gardens that have gone to seed, muddy soil that is too damp for growth, areas full of brambles and thorns and treacherous. Pluto can describe the dead plants in the yard, those that have gone black with brambling empty twigs or dead flowers. If Pluto indicates a flourishing garden, this would be one of brambles and thorns, such as roses (with thorns; not hybrids) and especially black roses, vining plants, especially those with thorns, cactus and plants such as spanish bayonet. These type of plants are thriving in a garden described by Pluto.

In business: Pluto describes all criminal businesses, including those run by mobsters, crooked politicians, murderers for hire as well as unethical investors and banksters and other greedy and violent people. Also people who are in positions of power and misuse that power and so also indicates dictators, warlords, revolutionary rulers and hellfire preachers and cult leaders. Pluto also signifies shops that sell sexual items for the more deviant among us, such as whips and handcuffs and other items used in S&M or for torture. Also shops that sell uncommon weapons, especially those that require violent contact, such as knives, swords, bats, flails, garottes, scythes, chains, handcuffs, iron maidens, etc.. Pluto rules archeology and so also rules over artifacts, ancient antiquities and heavy metals and, as such, also rules dealers in these items. Among more legitimate businesses indicated by Pluto are recyclers, trash collectors, landfill operators, junkyards, reclamation projects, city plumbing (water and sewer companies), bunker builders, companies that make construction equipment and earth moving machinery, gravediggers, funeral parlors, life insurance companies and sales people, probate courts and attorneys who specialize in the distribution of the goods of the dead. Estate managers.

Miscellaneous:

Physically, Pluto rules the sex organs (through Scorpio) but also the blood. It is involved in the transport of nutrients, bacterias, medications and any other element that changes the body, mostly through the veins and arteries. Rules the genitals specifically, the uterus, ovaries, testicles and prostate. Has providence over sexual diseases, both contagious and otherwise; cancer of the sex organs, infertility, miscarriage and abortion. It is responsible for the introduction of elements into the blood that cause diseases and toxic chemicals or drugs that are accidentally or unknowingly introduced to the body through the blood. Can indicate blood poisoning.

In describing the physical nature, it confers a heavy, square body shape that tends to become obese. Dark features, including dark hair and eyes and often a darkening of the skin of the face that can seem sinister. Shading around the eyes and undereye bags can make this person seem much older than he or she may be and can confer a shady or criminal appearance, whether the person is a criminal or not. Physical decadence similar to that of Neptune, drug and alcohol abuse and contempt for the care of the physical body. Disheveled and dirty. Small, square hands and feet; thick shoulders and midsection; large head. This person may be shorter than average.

Bringing The Elements Together

All of these descriptors are extremely valuable to you in your analysis of the forensic chart. By learning to blend the influences by assessing the quality of their placements and aspects will enable you to determine the location of events, the direction of any movements seen in the chart, which players are moving, how they are moving, where they are moving to and sometimes even why. You can tell if someone is in a car (or other vehicle), what direction they are moving in, the color of that car, the number of people in that car and how fast they are moving in the determined direction. You can even tell if the subject is restrained in the car or stuffed in the trunk. All of this and more can be determined using the indicators I have given you. You do not have to memorize this stuff because you can just keep the books and refer to them as you work. This is far easier than it was for me when I was learning; I had to memorize it because it was so cumbersome to find the right book and then even find the right information in that book. Most of the books I studied as a kid were out of print at that time. There are more books today but the information is far more scattered and you would have to own a lot of different books to get all the information I am giving you here. So don't lose this reference!

Let's look at the Lauren Spierer chart again and use what we've learned so far. Let's bring the elements together at this point and see what we can acheive.

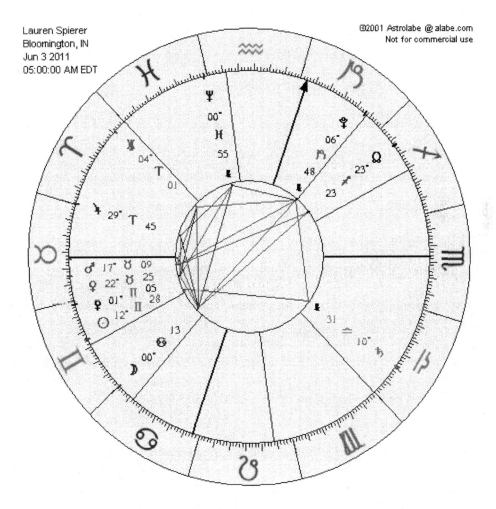

Lauren Spierer
Bloomington, IN
Jun 3 2011
05:00:00 AM EDT

This is not the chart for when Lauren was last seen. We presumably know what was going on when she was "last seen" by the witness. What we want to know is where she was going after she was last seen. So we use a chart for a half hour later, 5:00 AM. The first thing you have to do is isolate the subject. Lauren's marker will be the first house ruler. In this chart, the first house is Taurus with Venus in the first. This shows us that Lauren is still alive and moving under her own power. She has not be abducted or murdered yet. But notice that the seventh house is co ruled by Pluto and Mars. This is the person she is about to meet. Notice that Mars is right ahead of Venus in the first house. In fact, it is close to the Ascendant. This shows us this person (the seventh house ruler) facing her or, at the least, presenting himself to her. So this is where he appears. Just as an aside, if you look at the tables given to you in book one, you will see that Mars and Venus are very near to a fixed star known as Caput Algol. If you take a look at part eight of book one, you will see that Caput Algol is a violent fixed star that appears when brutal murders occur. Right away, this omen alone should have you worried about the outcome for Lauren Spierer. Still, the most important thing you can glean from this aspect, the joining of the first and seventh house rulers in the first house, is that the subject is about to meet her accoster. This is when and where it happens.

The idea of tracking movement in the charts is to determine the details of the when and where. If you refer to the tables I just gave you, you will see that Taurus often relates to hotels and resorts. So you might want to assume that Lauren was approached in an area near to a hotel or resort and possibly even the hotel where her abductor was staying at the time. Mars is disposed of by Venus so you can safely assume he is there for her; the dispositor of any planet shows you the planets purpose. In this case, his purpose was her. He was either looking for her or someone just like her. The actual area or location of the moment is shown best by the third house, which is the neighborhood. When the planets in question are not in the fourth or tenth houses (which show homes or businesses) then you can assume they are out and about. But where? With Cancer on the third house cusp and the Moon in Cancer, disposing of itself, you can also assume that they are somewhere near water. A hotel or resort near the water? Refer to the tables given for the Moon and for the sign Cancer. It could be a seafood restaurant near a hotel or a body of water behind a resort or a laundromat along a river. It's hard to say but you can say this; they are somewhere near water and probably a transient resort area with hotels or other short term rentals. Cancer is also on the fourth house cusp and since the fourth house describes Lauren's home, you can also safely assume she is not far from her own residence.

Now, from this, how do you determine distance and direction? Well, Taurus is a fixed sign so right away you can assume they do not travel far. Taurus is also an earth sign so it is possible both her and her abductor were on foot at the time. Earth signs often describing walking "on the ground". The neighborhood (third house) is described by Cancer (on the cusp) so refer to your tables for Cancer and note that this means they are traveling north. Moon is also in Cancer so this reinforces and does not mitigate the northerly direction. In some charts, you will find the Moon, the fourth house cusp and the third house ruler in different areas showing different directions. Those charts are harder to blend. But this one is singular in the northerly direction. So you can safely say that Lauren is moving north and she is not far from her own home. This area is near water and in an area with resorts, restaurants and hotels.

We have already noted that it seems that both people are on foot. But checking the ninth house (which is the third from the seventh and therefor shows us the abductors vehicle) we see that the ninth house ruler is Saturn in Libra. Saturn is in the sixth house. So perhaps he is driving a work vehicle? The sixth house applies to work. Adding to this, we can see that the co ruler of the seventh house is Pluto, also in the ninth house. Pluto describes a vehicle that is a bit battered perhaps and a darker color. The sign Capricorn describes colors like black or dark brown. Pluto is disposed of by Saturn, which supports the theory that the car is battered and older. It is a dark brown or black work vehicle that is battered and old; perhaps even rusty. Saturn in Libra could describe rusting areas with holes (for air to pass through). This is just one interpretation. And remember that I am not trying to hold your hand and make you see the charts my way but that I want you to open your own intuition and create your own analysis, using the standard guidelines. In this manner, Astrology is very much like Tarot. Use the symbols and interpret them your own way.

Moving along and trying to determine direction, we will have to blend the ninth and fourth houses. The ninth house is Capricorn, which opposes Cancer and gives us direction south. So now we have both north and south. Doesn't that mitigate the direction and change it? Not necessarily. In fact, it gives a different direction for the subject and the abductor. She is traveling north but the abductor is moving to the south. So he is coming from the north, heading south when he confronts her while she is going north. We know she is headed home and the charts show that her home is nearby but to the north so perhaps he is coming from her neighborhood? Perhaps he targeted her? It's hard to tell from what we've seen so far but it's possible. Keep your eye open for pointers that will confirm that. In the meantime, what you have so far is that Lauren was walking north when she was confronted by her abductor who was walking south. The markers in the ninth house indicate he had a work vehicle nearby. But the nature of Pluto in the ninth disposed of by Saturn in the sixth with both planets retrograde may indicate that the car was permanently parked or parked nearby for use in his work only. So if he had a work vehicle in this same area, what else might this tell you? Think about it.

We have the confrontation and assault of Lauren by this interloper. We need to move the charts forward to determine what happens in the next hour or so and then determine what direction they moved in after that.

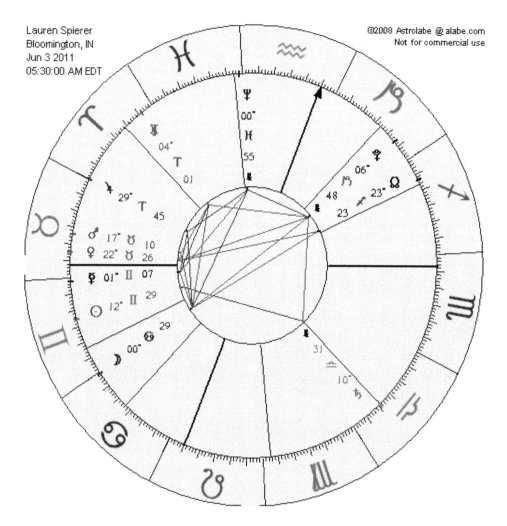

It is not my purpose here to re-address the Speirer case but to show you how to see directions and distance in a chart. In the chart for 5:30 AM, we see the two of them (Venus and Mars) in the twelfth house. The twelfth house faces in a southeasterly direction. As they move forward, the fourth house shows us their past location and the tenth house shows us their future location. This works well in forensic charts because the fourth house shows us the subject's neighborhood and this is where the event usually starts and the tenth house shows us the residence of the abductor, which is often where they end up. The tenth house ruler at this time is Uranus which is in the sign Aries in the eleventh house. We know that Aries refers to hideouts and places where criminals go. Uranus refers to airports, runways, air traffic control towers, airplanes and airplane hangers. Also, Uranus often describes electrical devices, radio stations, railway stations, railroad tracks, depots, workhouses and places of confinement.

Uranus also often refers to antique shops, radio and TV repair shops, radiologists offices and electrical engineering firms. Uranus here is disposed of by Mars in the twelfth and the twelfth house dovetails with Aquarius on places of confinement. So it can be assumed that Lauren was taken to a place where she was confined. Aries indicates east and the tenth house indicates south so perhaps they are moving in a southeasterly direction, which has already been indicated by the twelfth house.

Taking from all indicators, we can safely assume that after the attack, her abductor took Lauren southeast from where he found her.

Now, the next thing we would like to know is how far did he take her? In Astrology, time is the same as distance so you time movement using planetary distance. In this case, the fourth house ruler (the starting point) is the Sun in Gemini in the first house and the destination is ruled by the tenth so is shown by Uranus in Aries in the eleventh house. The distance from Uranus to the Sun is eight degrees (Sun in 12 degrees Gemini and Uranus in 4 degrees Aries). The Sun is the swifter moving planet and it is dexter so this slows things down. IF it had been sinister (applying to Uranus) it would be faster in motion. But the aspect is separating so you see it moving slower. Remember that, as a rule of thumb, that applying aspects (sinister in direction) move faster than those that are separating (dexter). We know, from the distance from one planet to the other, how long it takes to get from the starting point to the destination. Eight degrees. Aries is an angular sign while Gemini is cadent. The Sun is angular so it is swift in motion while Uranus is succeedent and slower. So we cannot say this was eight minutes. The movement just isn't fast enough. But we cannot say it was eight hours either because the motion is faster than that. So when you even it out, you might be able to say they traveled eight miles at whatever pace the speed limit allowed. It would be safe to say that in some areas they traveled faster than in others along the way.

Their method of travel appears to be described by Saturn in Libra. Saturn, as well as Mars, is disposed of by Venus, which rules the first house. This means we have to consider Venus as a marker in this event as well. Venus in Taurus describes a south by east direction. It is a succeedent sign in a cadent house so this slows it down even more. They did not take hours to get where they were going, but it wasn't done in a few minutes. They most likely traveled eight miles to where their destination and did so at varying speeds.

Tracking New Locations

Now that you know the direction they went in and, on average, how long it might have taken to travel how far, you will want to get an idea about the place they ended up in. The second location is often indicated by the tenth house, being that it describes the place of rest for the abductor. The ninth house has a role to play in this description, as well, being the third from the seventh and describing the neighborhood or general area. In this chart, we are studying Saturn and Uranus, as they rule the ninth and tenth houses, respectively. Saturn is in Libra and Uranus is in Aries, effectively opposite each other and actually only separated by six degrees. Oppositions in forensic charts describe conflict, confrontations, assaults, attacks, general unease and disagreements. In the case of locations, you might say that this aspect creates a problem for the abductor. Uranus in Aries describes places recently dug up or in chaos and where criminals or outlaws hang out. Saturn in Libra describes decorative areas that have been in place for a very long time. The opposition from these two planets for me describe a park or garden that is being renovated. But it can also mean a lovely, old apartment house that is being torn down. Or it can mean a once beautiful housing complex that has fallen into disarray and is being upgraded or torn down. This would create a conflict, no doubt, for anyone trying to roost here. Saturn in Libra is retrograde and in the fifth house while Uranus is in the eleventh so let's say that this place might be a party house or other place where people gather for unusual activities. Being that it is also defined by the sign Aries, it may be a party house being used by criminals or outlaws. Saturn in Libra may describe an older, once lovely, location that is now falling apart. When you notice that Neptune is in Pisces in the tenth house as well, you might think that this place is now inhabited by people with drug and drinking problems. Pisces rules medications and drugs while Neptune rules things that are hidden or beyond our eyes. So you may have a crackhouse in a previously nice area. This is what I might think looking at these aspects.

TRACKING MOVEMENTS IN THE CHART

Nailing Down Starting Points
(Determining Directional Movement From Starting Point)

Although we have used the fourth house in reviewing the one case so far, this is not always the starting point. You can't just go there every time. Depending upon the known facts, the event may have started almost anywhere. People are abducted from bars, from restaurants, from the side of the road. All of these elements have their own indicators and starting significators should be confined to the known facts. If the subject was nowhere near her home or neighborhood, then the fourth or third house will not work. In the Speirer case we knew that she was leaving a friends house and heading home and was not far from her home at the time. This is why we started where we did. So let's take a different case, a different chart and work on it. I am choosing the case of a girl who went missing, Theresa Hawley, because, for one, I have not done it on the blog and probably won't be doing it so there are no comparisons that can be drawn. I want you to start with a case you know nothing about. This case has also been solved and the girl was found alive so this is a chance to compare the charts to the known outcome and to see resolution in a case where the victim remains alive. Since this girl was last seen leaving home to meet someone for a date, she did not actually disappear from home but met this person elsewhere. It will be our job to figure out where that was and from where she disappeared and how she ended up where she did. Here is the chart for when she was last seen:

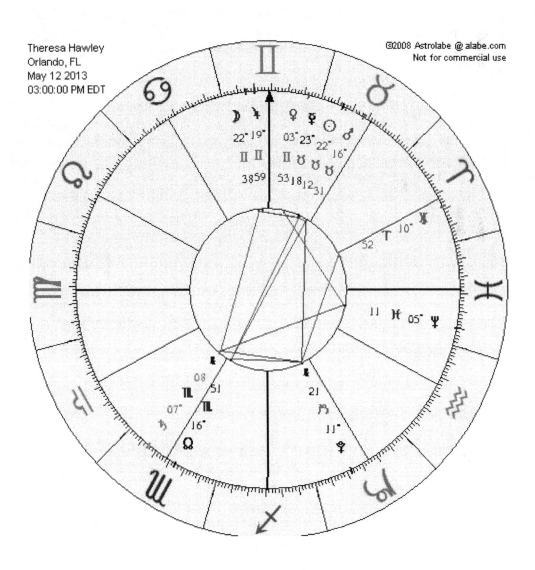

In order to follow Theresa's movements, we start with the first house ruler, which is her marker. We also look at the Moon, which co rules every chart. Here, we see that the first house ruler, Mercury, is in the ninth house. In these types of charts, the ninth house can mean many things but most often it refers to major highways, large transport vehicles, airplanes and other means of moving over a longer distance but it can also refer to the abductors car. It is the third house from the seventh and therefor describes the vehicle belonging to the "other person". In this chart, we see that the "other person" is ruled by Neptune (Pisces on the seventh cusp) and this planet is in the sixth in Pisces, which is in dignity. Mercury, Theresa's marker, is in conjunct the Sun, which rules the twelfth. It is true that no one knew who she was with nor where she went and that the car her "date" may have been driving is a mystery. Notice how her marker is tucked in with other planets, enough of them to be called a stellium, and that these other planets rule the twelfth, eighth and ninth houses. So we can assume that Theresa was picked up by this person and that she left in his car. These markers are present from the moment she was last seen alive.

The placement of the Moon in the tenth shows her to be out in the open, most likely on a public highway. The placement of the first house ruler in the ninth points to a major thoroughfare, either an interstate or a major highway system. So she met him on a large, public highway and not on the streets of her neighborhood or in a suburb. Perhaps she met him at an exit ramp? There are a lot of these along the major thoroughfares in the Orlando area. The placement of Neptune in the sixth tells us a few things about the person she met as well. This placement means he is "at work" in some capacity and could mean that he is active military. He could be in any arm of the armed services, but the sixth house most often refers to army or navy personnel and not such to air force or marines. There are naval stations all over Florida along the coasts but air force is more prominent in Orlando, which is in the center of the state. Otherwise, it can refer to traveling salespersons, business travelers who come to the area to conduct business, either in the short term or for longer periods. It can refer to someone who met her through his work and since they met on an online dating site, he may well be in the tech industry or conduct business on the web. An angular ruler in the sixth house also may refer to the fact that he will never be seen again. Especially so since the planet is Neptune.

So what is our concern right now? We are trying to figure out where she went and who with but it is important also how she gets there. We can see that she gets into a car and this is a great clue. Using the information given in the places and things section above, we can pin down what kind of car she got into. First of all, the ninth house ruler is Venus and it is in the sign Gemini. We know that Venus relates to a white color but also to a purple color and mixed together, this gives us a blue. We also know that Gemini relates to the color white but sometimes with a deep red or crimson mixed in. From this, I would extrapolate that the car was white, which is indicated by both significators. We also can see that Venus in Gemini is disposed of by Mercury in Taurus, also in the ninth house.

Venus relates to a more feminine vehicle and Mercury relates to something small and fast. So we are not talking about a truck or a van here. So this is probably a small luxury type vehicle in a white shade. It would be a fast car, too. Venus together with Mercury as a mix also gives us a purple or light purple mixture more towards a blue. So there may be a light purplish blue interior or seat covers of this color. Mercury and Venus are in mutual reception, which gives a sort of perfection in these charts so we might assume this was a new car or a car in really good shape; well cared for. It would give a great first impression for sure.

But the most important information given by these aspects and placements is the starting point for the event. We can see that the event started when she got into the strangers car for her "date". This occurred on a public thoroughfare such as a major highway system. These aspects, as we have observed them, have given us our "starting point".

Determining Directional Markers
(Comparing the Markers to Determine Movement)

Now, we want to know where they went, both in direction and actual place. We can do this by continuing to track the movements in this chart. The Moon, which is the chart co ruler, gives us more information on where Theresa might have gone. It is in the tenth house. This gives us two pieces of information. The sign Gemini in the tenth shows us a highway in an open space, such as a large highway that moves people from one part of the city to the other. Not a neighborhood road, a wooded path or anything like that. They are in his car on a major highway. But where are they headed? The third house shows us directional travel, especially in a vehicle. The sign on the third cusp is Scorpio, which gives directional north east. The house rulers are Pluto and Mars. Notice that Pluto is in the fourth house, which is directional north. Mars is in the sign Taurus which gives southeast. The ninth house, which is another directional marker, is occupied by Taurus, which, again is south east. The one consistent theme among all these markers is directional east. So we are going to say she traveled east with her "date".

And where are they headed? Notice that Jupiter, which rules the fourth house, is also in the tenth. The tenth is the fourth from the seventh and so they are headed to this man's home. Since the Moon and Jupiter are closely aligned I would say that Theresa went along with this for whatever reason she was given. And since both planets are disposed of by the first and tenth house rulers, I would say this would be their only destination. He was going to take her to his home and that was the only destination. To look for advanced planning in cases like these, check the nodes. The node here is in the third house directly opposing Mars, which rules the eighth house. This makes me think that this was thought about in advance but no real planning was involved. This is more like someone flying by the seat of their pants. I think he thought he would take his date back to his digs and then they'd move on or go out from there.

I do not see malevolent thoughts or schemes on the part of this man. By that I mean, nothing deviant or unusual. But one more thing stands out for me that might be useful if someone was trying to solve this case, Neptune is square to the ninth house ruler, Venus in Gemini. This seems to be showing us that he did not own this car, it was unfamiliar to him so this car was either a rental car, a borrowed car, a stolen car or a car belonging to someone else in his family. We have gathered a lot of information from the chart at this point and have also gleaned directional markers. From what we have seen so far, in the placements and aspects in this event chart, is that they traveled east by north. The charts have helped us to determine the directional markers.

Here is a report on the case from Scared Monkeys:

28 Year Old Theresa Hawley Missing Since May 12, 2013 in Orlando, FL ... After Date with Man She Met on Internet

28-year old Theresa Hawley was last seen Sunday afternoon, May 12, 2013 at about 3 p.m. when she told her friend she was going out on a date. She has not been heard from or seen since. Her roommates are concerned about her safety because they say she talked about meeting a man online. According to police she missing woman did not tell anyone who she was going out with or where. Co-workers called the police when Theresa Hawley didn't show up for work Monday morning at Uptown Dog in Winter Park where she worked as a dog groomer for the past three years. Presently her cell phone goes straight to voicemail.

Orlando Police say Theresa Hawley, 28, hasn't been seen since Sunday afternoon, after she told her friends she was going out on a date.

"She was innocently just thinking that somebody's going to take me out, finally I get to go out on a date, you know, and that's all she was thinking, she hasn't been back, we haven't had any phone calls," said Hawley's roommate Mary Cosme.

Her roommates are concerned about her safety because they say she talked about meeting a man online — they don't know if someone picked her up or if she met them, but they say she didn't take any clothes or belongings with her, only her wallet and cell phone, which they say is now going straight to voicemail.

Progressing the Chart Hour by Hour

In order to discover what else happened that night, after she was taken on this date, we have to run the charts forward. This is a method of analyzing forensic charts that I invented. I consider my method to be currently still in "beta" mode.

Many Astrologers would scratch their head if they saw me doing this and would, no doubt, think it was more metaphysical than scientific. Other Astrologers might find it interesting and try it. But it is, as of yet, unproven and still in development. What I did was meld a few systems together because it just made sense to do so. If you can ask any question in a horary and draw up a chart for the moment the question was asked, then you should be able to ask about times and places as well. You should be able to ask what happened at a certain hour and draw up a chart for that hour and read it as easily as you would the chart for the time the question was asked. In fact, it should be closer to the truth. If you can draw a chart for a time and place of birth and, from there, extrapolate the outcome of an entire life that lasts over 50 years, then you should be able to draw up a birth chart for an event and do the same thing. And, if you can progress a chart month to month or year to year then you should be able to do it minute by minute, hour by hour and day by day as well. It's as simple as that to my way of thinking and so this method of progressing horary charts came to be. I want you to treat it as an experiment. Learn it, use it and see if you can't perfect it using your own talents, insights and understandings. I see it as an open door to astrological insight and hope you can use it in that manner as well.

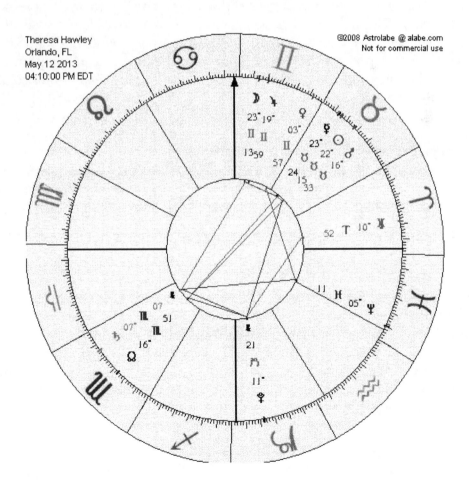

Back to the chart. Just after 4 pm Libra moves onto the Ascendant, making Venus the new chart ruler. This doesn't really change the charts much because the previous chart ruler, Mercury, was conjunct Venus at that time. In this next chart, Venus is in the ninth house in the same manner that Mercury was in the ninth previously and shows us that her situation hasn't changed. She is still with this man; the Moon, the chart co ruler, has now moved into the ninth house from the tenth, so it is probable they are in the car and the car is parked. The Moon rules the tenth house and it is currently in the ninth, so this might indicate a garage or parking spot in front of or adjacent to a public facility. Remember that the tenth house is the fourth from the seventh and that the ninth is the third from the seventh; Gemini echoes this scenario as it also rules parking lots, garages and vehicle storage areas. These are my ideas and impressions but feel free to refer to the places and things section earlier in the book to come up with your own that may well be different than mine. I am just showing you how I work with the charts to come up with the tracking information that I do. Where do you think they are at this point?

There is one interesting and influencial change in placement and aspect here that I have to point out. The node, in the second house now, is opposed to Mars in the eighth. Mars is the seventh house ruler in this chart, which shows us an energy exchange between the node and the ruler. This indicates a "fast cooked" plan on the fly. He has suddenly come up with a scheme of some sort. So perhaps this is the purpose in moving her to the car and then parking somewhere. This chart also seems to describe a sexual proposition. Mars in the eighth in conjunction with the eleventh house ruler. This shows sexual energy. Not the romantic kind but the "I just met you and this is just a hit and run" kind of sex. This is shown by the eleventh house ruler in the eighth. Also, the fifth house ruler is in the seventh house, describing the motivations of the other person, which appear to be sexual in nature. Pluto is also angular in the fourth house and any time Pluto is angular, you need to look for indicators of chaos, disruption, disaster, change and violence. In addition, Saturn and Pluto are in mutual reception from the second to the fourth houses, which gives these planets added strength. With Saturn so close to the node in Scorpio, the implication of a plot or a scheme again appears. But the positive aspects between these planets reduces the probability of violence. Both of these planets are retrograde so this may be a proposition that is rather subtle or not overly aggressive. In an event like this, where a stranger has groomed and seduced a young woman online and then gotten control over her by picking her up in his car, a horrible outcome is presupposed. She is at his mercy from the very first moment. That is played out in the chart aspects as well and now the charts are showing us that he has taken her somewhere in the car, parked and made a sexual "pass". The best part of this is that the charts do not support violence or rape. The aspects between planets are positive, including mutual reception between Saturn and Pluto, showing self control, and the Moon is conjoined Jupiter, showing good will and basically good feelings.

Remember our earlier findings. He is driving a light colored car that may be a rental or a stolen car and they traveled west by south on a major thoroughfare when they left her home. We also find that they have traveled east and then parked outside of a store or other business. At this point, we see that he is making sexual overtures to her but not violent ones, as the planets involved are retrograde and well aspected. So what happens now?

Now we need to move on to the next time in the event and see what happens.

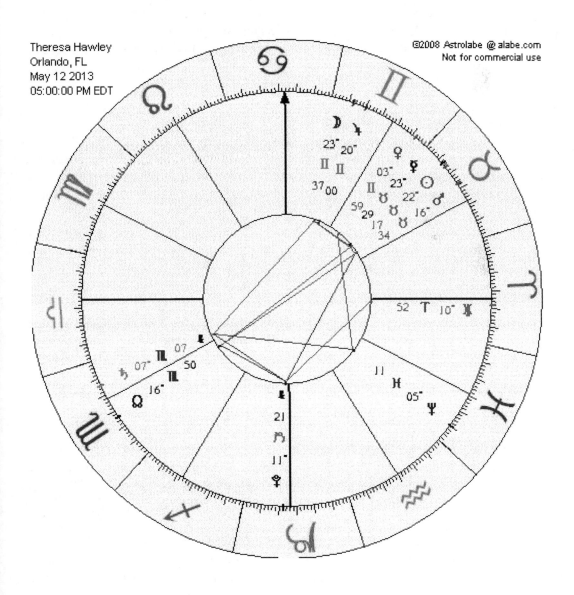

The first thing that stands out in this chart is the stellium of planets in the eighth house. If you refer to book one and check out the positions of the fixed stars and their meanings you will see that both Caput Algol and the Pleiades are in the eighth house of death near to a group of planets. They are not conjoined the first house ruler nor to any angular planets but these fixed stars are so violent and dangerous that their mere presence in the eighth house should be noted and watched with great care. But because they are not angular and are not aspected to any ruling planets, we can say that they are not a driving force in this event. Although there appears to be a beginning death pattern, we are not going to say that this was necessarily brutal or violent. We are not able to say that Theresa is dead yet either as the death pattern is small and unformed. However, you must also note the presence of Saturn in the first house and the probability that it will move into the twelfth in the next hour or so. This, too, must be noted and watched. These are the elements that will help you to determine if the subject is dead or alive. So far, these charts show her alive.

Progressing the Chart Over Longer Periods

Continuing with the task of moving the event forward and tracking what these people are doing, I will point out that Mars, the seventh house ruler, is still in the eighth and it is still conjunct to the eleventh house ruler, so the sexual markers are still present. This does not mean, however, that he assaulted her.

I must point out, for your future reference in reading other charts, when sexual markers show up in more than one chart, this is a guarantee it happened. If it only appears in one chart and then disappears, it can mean sex was only a thought or it was attempted and thwarted somehow. In this case, it appears to have gone on unchallenged. Besides, not only are these aspects involving the eighth and eleventh houses, both sex houses, but the axis created by the opposition from the node to Mars involves the signs Taurus and Scorpio, the most sexual signs in the Zodiac. This alone makes me believe he hoped to have sex with whatever girl he got to meet him for a date. This was his game plan. He may not have had a specific plan for Theresa and he may not have stalked her exclusively but he was trolling for a new victim when he was hanging out on that dating site. But I do not see violent rape. I see coercion, perhaps, or even a little intimidation (Venus square Neptune) but nothing bloody or brutal. I think she felt pressured to have sexual contact or perhaps did not know how to refuse and so something happened. It may have been limited in nature, something short of intercourse, perhaps, but some sort of sexual contact is indicated in the charts we have seen.

NOTE: In relation to time and spans of time: You have to remember that time on Earth is an illusion and time in space is distance. So true time is in the measure of distance from one event to another so this may have happened in an instant... or in a few minutes... and appear to have lasted for hours. You must remember that time cannot be assessed using Astrology in this manner. All you can say is what happened. Not how long it went on or at what time it began or ended. Time on Earth is a vantage point, nothing more. Now that you have digested that I must say that at this point in the analysis, you might end up running through charts pretty quickly, getting a bit of information from each as you go. This makes it appear that the event went on for hours and that a subject was raped or killed at a certain time. Again, I must warn you against this type of thinking. We are talking about an event that has no seperation, is not at a distance from a parallel event, and so it is uniform in time and distance. This probably all happened in a very short period of time, even though it takes charts drawn for several hours to glean all the facts. So bear with me.

We are trying to track movements in this event and we are sort of stuck right now. He is making propositions to her in a parked car somewhere and the fact that this has shown up in two charts so far we know it has happened. In the second chart, the one for 5 pm, we are doubling down on the location as well. The Moon, which rules the tenth house and also co rules the subject in question, is still in the ninth house, showing a parked vehicle in an outdoor location. You can get more clues from the placement of the third and fourth house rulers, which will show you the neighborhood. The fourth house ruler in the first shows us that this is north east of Theresa's home (the fourth house shows north and Scorpio shows us north by east). The third house ruler will show you even more about the neighborhood and since it is placed in the ninth, we see that the area outdoors is in a commercial area (the third often describes business districts) near a highway or thoroughfare (the ninth house again). The Moon is conjunct Jupiter, which rules the third house, showing us continuity between her neighborhood and this area, basically drawing a line traveling east from where they started to this location, along a major highway. The Moon with Jupiter in Gemini also points to commercial areas, with cars zipping by and people around. They are NOT hiding in the woods somewhere or tucked away in a dark apartment.

But you should also note that the Moon, which rules his current residence (the Moon rules the tenth and the tenth is the fourth from the seventh), is in the sign Gemini. Gemini is ruled by Mercury and often describes short term rentals, timeshares, vacation homes, second homes, mobile homes, trailers and any home that can be moved from place to place or is moved in and out of in a short period of time. It does not, however, rule hotels, which belong to the providence of Venus and the sign Taurus nor does it rule luxury apartments, condos or penthouses, which are all ruled by the Sun and the sign Leo. But small, roadside motels with few amenities and that are often used by traveling businessmen can be associated with Mercury and the signs Gemini and Virgo. So this man may have been staying nearby but does not actually live there year round. This, along with the node's position, as discussed earlier, shows us some degree of pre planning, perhaps, if we are to assume that he rented a room after he made the date with this girl. Orlando is a vacation town and there are plenty of motels and short term rentals to be had year round and at a last minute. So keep this in mind when analyzing this case and looking for answers.

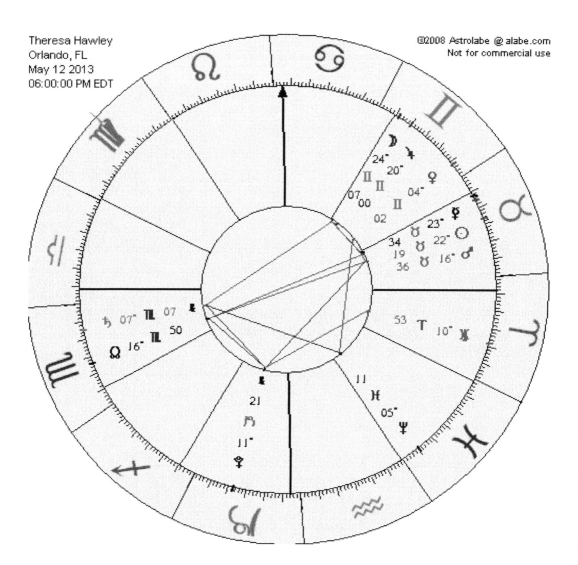

Tracking Movement Through the Event

This chart is going to show you what happened next. I want you to look closely at these charts as I point out how some leading indicators can be offset by aspects or house placements. This chart appears to show us a death pattern. In fact, it is a strong one. The first house ruler, Venus, and the Moon are together in the eighth house of death. Saturn in Scorpio is rising in the first house, closing in on the Ascendant. And all of these indicators are leading the chart and describing a pattern I often assign as death. But there are mitigating factors here and I want you to see them so you will not miss them in the future, when you are working on charts that are meant to help others locate missing persons. Saturn, which rules the bones and the body, is in the first house in the sign Scorpio, which rules the eighth house, the house of death, in the natural zodiac. Another factor is the first house ruler, Venus, which is in the eighth house along with the chart co ruler, the Moon. The fourth house ruler is Saturn. These indicators could have you proclaiming this person as dead, no? In fact, the chart looks like this subject is going to be a "dead body". This would easily be assumed by someone who hasn't seen a lot of charts or even by someone like myself, who has read hundreds, and just falls into a lazy mode. But there are mitigating factors that cannot be ignored.

First of all, there is nothing in the twelfth house. And when Saturn finally makes it to the twelfth house (rolling the charts forward to the next hour, for instance) only the Moon remains in the eighth house and the first house ruler will be in the seventh. You need angular planets in the twelfth house, ideally the first house ruler, the Moon, the fifth house ruler (if the subject is a child) or the dispositor of the Moon. You need something in the twelfth supporting other planets in the eighth AT THE SAME TIME. Also, the fourth house ruler should also be in play. The fourth house shows the place of death as well as the burial site or grave. When Saturn finally moves into the twelfth house, it no longer rules the fourth house. Saturn disposes of Pluto in Capricorn and is in mutual reception with Pluto at the same time. And Pluto is going to be the first house ruler from the third house, not the fourth. At that point, Mars co rules the first house also but it is in the seventh house, not a death house. Also, the fourth house ruler is now Uranus, positioned in the fifth house, where it is disposed of by Mars in the seventh. And both the first and seventh house rulers, Mars and Venus, respectively, are in the seventh house, not a death house. These indicators show a confrontation of sorts, perhaps an outright rejection from one to the other and the possibility that they may have argued, but no signs of violence and whatever death pattern seemed to be forming has now disappeared. There is no support for a conclusion of death in this case. The only thing here is a sexual advance and perhaps sexual contact. But even that appears to be subtle manipulation, not violent rape.

Now, at this point I want to tell you that this girl was found alive. She was taken to a nearby city on the east coast of the state, which is served by a major highway system. She was dumped in a convenience store parking lot, from where she called her mother. She is now home, safe and sound, but she did have a bad experience. Nothing more has come out about this case so it is one for the doing and watching. Study it for yourself and come to your own conclusions about what happened to Theresa. She is being mysterious about details of this case so perhaps you can find her motives and what happened that she isn't saying. The sexual contact I have shown you in these charts could be a source of embarassment for her. What do you think happened here? When you put together your own analysis, you can then compare it to the facts as they emerge (if and when they do). From those facts, you can learn more about how to read these charts in the future.

I want to mention one more thing to you as you embark upon this study. You will find that you are not right all of the time and that your analysis will fall short on many details. Do not lose heart. I have been criticized, accused of being a fraud, accused of trying to rob people of their money (which is why I do most of my work for free), called a sham and a hustler, etc... and there are many people who dismiss metaphysical work and look for any opportunity to make you look foolish. The police don't take this stuff seriously, although you may find, as you get better at this, that they are willing to look at anything when the case has gone stone cold. But you should never let your failures get you down. There is simply more work to be done. Do not be too willing to dismiss your own work in this manner just because you gave someone else ammunition to shoot you down. Hopefully you learn from your mistakes and then just get back at it, getting better at it with every effort. It has to be completely disproven, shown to not work at all repeatedly, before I will set it aside and leave it to the history books. So far, that has not been the case. It has proven to be correct in far too many details and even, in some cases, in every small detail. Although there are also other small details that just don't fit, the preponderance of correct information makes it a study worth time and effort. So keep your chin up even if you fall on your face once in a while.

I will not be doing the Theresa Hawley case on the blog so this is yours alone to work on. You can keep my findings and then work on it to develop your own theories. When they solve the case, you can privately compare what I found, what you found, and what really happened. It should be a great tool for you to use in your study.

Timing Events in the Chart

Timing Events in the Chart Using Planets in Signs and Houses:

Each house in the natural zodiac is assigned a quality, which indicates the speed of aspects as they occur in that house. Every sign has a quality that is similar to those of the houses and is used to determine the forward motion of those planets as they travel through the natural zodiac. These qualities have been perfected by the masters of horary divination using astrology charts. You can refer to any book on horary astrology to gather information about the qualities of houses and signs as they apply to the timing of events. Here are some charts you can use as well:

CHART: Qualities of the Houses

HOUSE -QUALITY-MEASURE OF TIME

1 - Angular - Minutes to Hours
2 - Succeedent - Days to Weeks
3 - Cadent - Months to Years
4 - Angular - Minutes to Hours
5 - Succeedent- Days to Weeks
6 - Cadent - Months to Years
7 - Angular - Minutes to Hours
8 - Succeedent - Days to Weeks
9 - Cadent - Months to Years
10- Angular - Minutes to Hours
11 - Succeedent - Days to Weeks
12 - Cadent - Months to Years

CHART: Qualities of the Signs

SIGN - QUALITY - MEASURE OF TIME

Aries - Cardinal - Minutes to Hours
Taurus - Fixed - Months to Years
Gemini - Mutable - Days to Weeks
Cancer - Cardinal - Minutes to Hours
Leo - Fixed - Months to Years
Virgo - Mutable - Days to Weeks
Libra - Cardinal - Minutes to Hours
Scorpio - Fixed - Months to Years
Sagittarius - Mutable - Days to Weeks
Capricorn - Cardinal - Minutes to Hours
Aquarius - Fixed - Months to Years
Pisces - Mutable - Days to Weeks

These charts should provide quick reference when you are trying to assess the passage of time in a chart. Remember, however, that timing is tricky when you are reflecting time in space back to time on Earth. Do not just jump on a number because it appears to fit the time given in an event. Charts can be drawn over a few hours and actually reflect the events of the next several months.

You know this because you draw up birth charts and use them to predict the outcome of a life that may last 90 years. But pin pointing exact times and dates of the events you predict is extremely difficult. In most events, you will give a general description of the time involved, whether it's hours, days or months. Sometimes the case isn't solved for years and the body is never found. You have to be open to this if you want to use these charts to help investigators.

In most cases, the chart drawn for the time last seen will give you everything you are looking for. However, the timing will be way off. This is because the chart will show the subject is dead but there is no way of telling when that happened. In those cases, you will use directional markers and timing elements to help investigators figure out what direction they went and how far or how long it took in order to try to locate the body. Again, this will always be general and cannot be exact. You may be able to tell that they traveled west from the original location and that they traveled for as long as a few hours, for instance. This would help determine how far away they went in a certain direction, helping narrow down destinations. Although time doesn't matter much is the course of events, it can be used to locate burial sites or where someone may be held prisoner. I will show you how as we move forward in this book.

At this point, you need to familiarize yourself with the qualities of each sign and house and how this translates into time. You will learn, after practice, how to blend these influences and come up with a plausible window of time. You can then use this measure of time to determine how long and how far. Along with directional markers, as pointed out earlier, this measure of time can help a lot when attempting to find a missing person.

Timing Events in the Chart Using Planetary Motion

You can determine general windows of time pretty easily by assessing the planets and their forward motion. When a planet is retrograde, for instance, or stationary, then the events in question drag on much longer than ordinary and may even cause events to remain stagnant for years. By counting the days it will take for the planet to go direct you can assess just how many years it may be before the subject is found or the case is solved. On the other hand, when you see that the planetary motion is rapid, then the timing of events is greatly reduced and may indicate that everything happened swiftly. When the charts show you the timing involved, you should accept this and pass it on to those who need the information and not make attempts to change the outcome with other predictions. You should always give information to the investigators or interested parties the window of time you discover and any other clues you may unearth. But don't assume that the clues you find will solve the crime any sooner than the charts predict.

CHART: Daily Motion of Planets

PLANET	DAILY MOTION
The Sun	59 minutes - 1 degree a day
The Moon	12-15 degrees a day
Mercury	1 degree 6 minutes - 1 degree 40 minutes a day
Venus	1 degree 2 minutes - 1 degree 22 minutes a day
Mars	31 - 45 minutes a day
Jupiter	5 - 15 minutes a day
Saturn	2 minutes a day
Uranus	1 minute a day
Neptune	Less than a minute a day
Pluto	Less than a minute a day

This chart shows the natural daily motion of the planets as they move through the natural zodiac. The time spread given for the planetary motion is absolute. The lowest number being the slowest motion of that planet and the highest being the swiftest. You will want to make note of the motion as given in the ephemeris when you draw up the event chart. The current motion of the planets will help you determine, right off the bat, if this event occurred over a short, swift period of time or if it was dragged out and may take years. It will be from this starting point, that you will use the charts you draw up, with the houses and planetary placements, to blend all the factors and come up with a reasonable window of time for any activity you are trying to track.

I will use a sample chart as an example for you to study. I want to use the Theresa Hawley case again because it has been solved so it will be easier to demonstrate what I'm talking about. We know that the girl went on a date on May 12 but wasn't recovered for a week. Since we would not know the recovery date and time in a case we would be analyzing, we would be using the chart for the time last seen as our guide. From that chart, we should be able to determine the movements and the window of time for all expected events. We have already determined the direction in the previous section, which was northeast. This is also born out by the known facts, that she was picked up in DeBary, a town on the east coast just north of Orlando. We also know that she was picked up in a public location near a commercial district, shown in the previous charts. The known facts are that she was picked up in a convenience store that was on the same property as a strip mall. We do not know what happened to her and even though the charts show sexual activity we cannot verify this from the reports. She has not said much about what happened except to say that it was a "bad experience". So the charts we have assessed, for distance and location, appear to be supported by the now known facts. So let's see if we can't determine time from this chart as well.

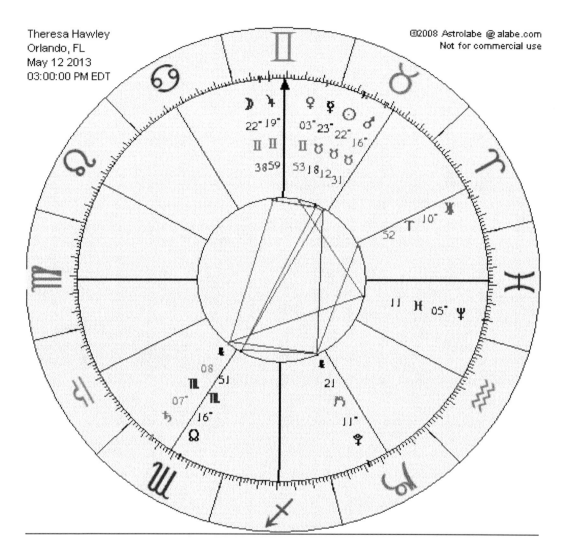

Timing markers are usually those planets and houses that would normally indicate direction and speed. The third house and ninth house give us movement through travel and can be used to determine the speed and distance of a vehicle in motion. The tenth house and fourth house are locational markers and can help us determine the time it takes to get from an abduction site to the final destination. They are helpful in locating where people are being held captive or where dead bodies are buried. They can also show us where runaways end up or where people may be left after an event, such as this one. It is the tenth and fourth house markers that allowed us to determine her final location which was a public place in a commercial district. But this girl was held for several days. Where in the chart can we determine that length of time and predict it? First of all, you would try to determine the distance from the girl to her home. I mean this in terms of time and space not spatial distance. So you will now attempt to use her first house marker, Mercury, and consider it in relation to the fourth house marker, Jupiter. There is no aspect between them in this chart, which is a sign that she won't be returning quickly. In fact, Mercury is in a fixed sign (Taurus) which shows that time will be extended. So we know, from this alone, that she won't be returned this same night and probably not the next few days. Jupiter is angular in a mutable sign, however, so this shortens the period by weeks to probably days rather than extending it out to months, as a fixed sign might indicate, especially in a fixed or succeedent house. But the fourth house ruler is angular in a mutable sign, which gives us a small but considerable clue that she will be returning home eventually. Especially since none of the markers for the subject are in the eighth house (indicating death), the twelfth house (indicating imprisonment) or the sixth house (indicating disappearance). In fact, the Moon and Mercury are above the horizon, which is another marker for possible recovery. And since Mercury is in a fixed sign, Taurus, and not aspecting Jupiter, we might be quick to assume it will be months before she is found. But what is the speed of Mercury and Jupiter in these charts, at this time? This will help you a lot.

Get out your ephemeris. Look up May 2013 and locate Mercury. Notice how fast Mercury is in forward motion at this time. It is moving at a rate of 2 degrees a day. It is also direct the entire month and does not retrograde. Jupiter is moving at a rate of 2 degrees a week on average. So when do these two planets finally come together? ON MAY 27, 2013. Count it out yourself and check the ephemeris. This is the EXACT day when both Jupiter and Mercury (the planets ruling the fourth and tenth houses respectively, in the event chart) conjoin at 23 degrees Gemini. This is the day she was discovered. So the whole thing fits perfectly and if you worked your charts the right way, you would be able to predict her recovery within two weeks... or even for exactly May 27, the day she was found.

Timing Events in the Chart Using Signs on House Cusps

Now that we have covered using the houses and house rulers to determine speed, let's use the signs on the cusps of the houses to affirm or deny what we have already found. In this case, we have determined the discovery to be in two weeks.

The signs in question in this chart are Virgo (first house rulership) and Sagittarius (fourth house rulership). You are trying to find out when the person or body will be recovered, if ever. Virgo is a mutable sign and gives days to weeks. Ditto for Sagittarius. So how many days or weeks? Since each of these cusps are at 15 degrees of these signs we can assume it will take 15 degrees for them to clear the cusp. We can then assume it might take 15 days to recover the subject.

This may look really simple on the surface but it is not. It is just not always the case that the first and fourth house rulers are in the exact same degree of their respective signs. It is also not always a given that they will be in signs of the same quality. Just because they are 90 degrees apart does not guarantee this placement. Interception is a factor in many charts that are done and even in this chart you can see that other house cusps are in different degrees although I must admit this is the closest I have seen a time chart come to being an equal house chart. Equal house charts are called solar charts because they reflect only the position of the Sun on a particular date and not the time of the event (or birth). Charts based on the time of events (or births) are called natal or event charts. Charts based on time are the only truly accurate charts in my humble opinion. Equal house charts based on the movements of the Sun are too arbitrary and do not give a lot of detail. So it not that common for event charts based on time to come this close to being equal in house placements. But this chart does have a lot of houses placed in the same degree of signs and there is no interception. So please remember that, as clear as this example has turned out to be, it is not that common. All you have to do to see this more clearly is to revisit the charts for Lauren Spierer given earlier in this book. There you can see examples of house cusps in varying degrees of signs and the interception of signs in singular houses. In this chart you also have signs that do not occupy a house cusp. This type of variation is far more common than the placements seen in the Hawley case. But I used it for that reason. It makes everything clear.

Bringing Timing and Distance Together

This is the hardest thing you will have to do with your results. Bringing them together to give a total picture is difficult even for experienced astrologers. I have trouble with it and sometimes don't do it at all. But this is the coup de gras in those cases where you are trying to help investigators recover a missing person, dead or alive. Of course, the circumstances will vary, depending on whether the chart shows the subject to be dead or alive. If the person has been murdered and you know them to be dead, then you need to ascertain whether the body is buried, left out in the open, near water or on open land, etc... and you will do this using the markers given in this book. I will show you how to do that in a moment. From that knowledge, that the body is buried or left in the water or whatever, you then using timing and distance to determine the local area where this may be. You will also use maps. The beginning stages of this are simple but the wrap up is insanely hard. In the beginning stages, you first determine what the local markers are and from there, locate on a map areas in the local area that meet this definition. For instance, you see that the body has been dropped in the water and that the body of water is not large and may be a lake or a pond. Add to this knowledge, your directional markers you have gathered from the charts as shown above and then get out the maps. Look in that direction from the area on the map you know the subject was last seen and move in that direction on the map until you locate bodies of water that match this description. Aha! You think now I will just find her. It's just that simple. Oh, but it's not!

Once you have located bodies of water on the map, you will also get a lesson in nature. Nature tends to create more than one land formation in an area that is predisposed to such locations. What I mean by this is if there is one pond there is likely more. If there is one desert area then there is probably many more, including vast expanses that go on for miles. Now, what do you do with that? You went east on the map and found a pond but if you look around there are other lakes and ponds also continuing east. This is where the timing markers may or may not be handy. Given that you can narrow down the time to minutes or hours and determine the speed that vehicles go in such an area, you might be able to determine which of these ponds may be viable. You may also find that several of the ponds or lakes fit the time and distance evaluation. So now what? You will have to go back to your descriptors and begin shuffling through them until you find distinctive markers in a particular area that fit. This could be something as simple as a small body of water that is very deep (such as with Neptune, Jupiter or Pisces markers) or a shallow body (such as with Mercury or Venus markers in water signs). Or you might find that the desert isn't sandy much but filled with rocks and craggy, such as you would find with markers in Capricorn or Saturn in an earth sign as a marker. You are going to have to dig through these variables and then match them to the bodies of water on your list. And it isn't easy.

Let me give you an example. I want to use a chart where the body was found.

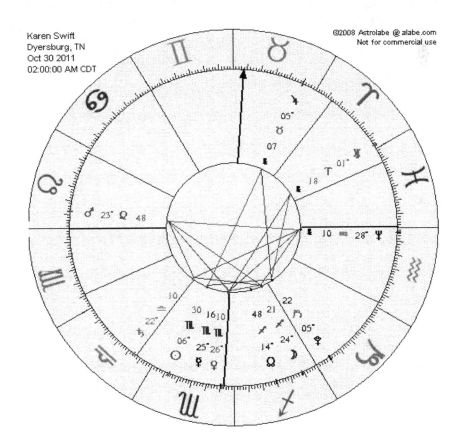

This is the Karen Swift case and this chart is for the time she was last seen. Remember that you can find out everything you need to know from the chart drawn for the time the subject was last seen. Moving the charts forward simply sheds light on certain factors, either supporting conclusions or adding to them. There are also times when you study the heck out of the chart and just don't find what you are looking for. Supporting charts for the next few hours will sometimes give you that.

I chose the Swift case because her body was found and we can use that to demonstrate the facts the charts reveal. I do realize that hindsight is 20/20 and that it is very hard to get that vision beforehand, especially when so little is known about the circumstances in most of these cases. But hopefully we can study these charts, compare them with the known facts and learn how to discern.

Although this chart does not render a death pattern and leaves us wondering if she is still alive, it does show an attack on this woman with Mars at the first cusp. Noting that Mars is disposed of by the Sun in the third house we might assume she was attacked while she was in her car. This was not an accident, it would seem, because Mars indicates a personal attack. Uranus or Mercury might be present at an accident. Notice how Neptune rules her seventh house cusp and is disposed of by Uranus in the eighth. There is something secretive about this person she is with; she either with a lover other than her estranged husband or she is sneaking around still having sex with that estranged husband. Either way, this is a secret affair (Neptune and the sign Pisces ruling the eighth house cusp). Notice also that the first house ruler, Mercury, is in Scorpio in the third and disposed of by Pluto in the fifth. There was a sexual encounter in and among the other circumstances surrounding this woman's evening.

But now she has disappeared and where and when will they find her? Notice that the first house ruler, tenth house ruler and twelfth house ruler are all in the third house in Scorpio. For one thing, this tells us that whether she is dead or alive she not far from her own neighborhood. It also means that somehow her car is involved. Notice that the first house ruler, Mercury, is only a degree away from the tenth house ruler, Venus. They are in the sign Scorpio. Checking the places and things associated with Scorpio, we find that she might be in a dirty, swampy place like a vineyard or a compost heap. She might also be found in a place of mourning or greiving, such as a graveyard. Scorpio also relates to cemetaries. This is an obscured place, dark and dirty and not easily seen. All of this not far from her home.

The facts bear out that her car was found a mile from her home. The first house ruler is only 1 degree away from the tenth house ruler, making the distance from her home about a mile. This is her neighborhood. The body was not far from her car. She was covered with vines in a dirty area near the highway and her body was on property belonging to a cemetary (or graveyard). Pretty simple, no? It can be this simple when you know where to look.

PRACTICE CHARTS-

Two Unsolved Cold Cases

I have two cases that I have been working on for several years. They are, as of yet, unsolved and very cold. They are both in my backyard, so I can give you the whole story to help you in your analysis. But they make a good background for charting because no one is working these cases anymore and there hasn't been anything new on either one in years. I will show you the charts I have drawn up for these cases and give you a running start on the analysis. I don't expect you to solve these (although that would be awesome if someone did) but to practice your analysis of the charts using the details of these cases.

The first case is for a young boy who disappeared while hitchiking home from his girlfriend's home. Hitchhiking was a common practice in Florida in the 1970s and the city this boy lived in, Cocoa Beach, was a hub for visitors from all walks of life. This case has been considered closed by the CBPD because they just decided to blame a now dead serial killer for it and leave it at that. I won't comment on how lazy the CBPD was at that time and how few murders actually occurred in the area, leaving them short on experience to boot. They wanted to just say he ran away but the details just didn't match it. There is no doubt he disappeared while hitchhiking home that day and no one really knows what happened to him. Here is the chart for the time he was last seen:

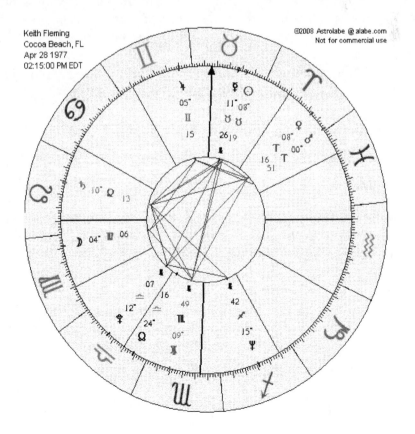

Since his parents picked him up at school and then took him to a girlfriends home and dropped him off, the time when they dropped him off is the time he was last seen by a verifiable witness. I know it had to be around 2:15 PM because I live in the area and I am very familiar with the distance they traveled from the school to the girls home. School let out at 2 pm in 1977.

Here is an excerpt from The Charley Project
(http://www.charleyproject.org/cases/f/fleming_keith.html)

"Fleming was last seen walking home from his girlfriend's house in Cocoa Beach, Florida on April 28, 1977. His parents had dropped him off at the girlfriend's residence after school and he was supposed to be back home for dinner. He left the residence with his girlfriend and they rode on her bicycle to the end of Osceola Street at State Road A1A. Then Fleming got off and said he was going to hitchhike the rest of the way home, which was a common practice by Cocoa Beach residents at the time. He never arrived home and has never been heard seen or heard from again. He was last seen wearing a t-shirt, thong sandals and a gold chain with an Italian horn."

The horrible lack of interest in this case by the CBPD is legendary. The girl who last saw Fleming was not even interviewed until 1993, over two decades later and most probably after she had forgotten important details that will now never be recovered. The PD dismissed him as a runaway and went to lunch. As a result, no one knows the color of the t shirt he was wearing, whether he had on shorts or jeans, etc... His parents have not been good sources of information. His father has since died but his mother and brother continue to hold out hope and keep up the search. There is so little information about this case that even the timeline is pretty much unknown, except for the fact that his parents dropped him off right after school, sometime between 2 and 2:30 pm.

Looking at the chart I see a few things that dovetail with the few facts we have. You need to always try to match the charts with the reported facts to be good and sure the charts are viable. There are going to be many occassions where the charts are not; many of them end up being unreadable. First of all, this chart has Virgo on the first house cusp with the Moon in Virgo. Strangely enough, Keith was a Virgo (BD Sept 18, 1963). You can see in this chart, his mother (and father reportedly) ruled by the seventh house ruler, Uranus in the third. She is in her car. Mercury, which rules all children, is in the ninth, showing a child at school. Mercury is conjunct the Sun, which rules the first house, so this child is Keith. The Sun in the ninth also shows the child in the parents car (ninth being the third from the seventh). The fifth house ruler, Jupiter, which co rules the child, is in the tenth. So he he is on the way to someone else's home. This chart seems to fit the facts we've been given so we'll call it viable. We will also assume, from this chart, that the parents told everyone the truth.

There are some ominous aspects in this chart that I want to point out to you, the student. These are the aspects that will require watching as you progress the charts forward. The Moon, which rules the child, is in the first house in the same sign as the boy's birth sign, Virgo. But it is rising towards the twelfth house and this has to be watched. At the same time, Pluto, which sits quietly in the second, will become angular within an hour or so as it clocks into the first house. This also is worth paying attention to. Also, Venus and Mars are cloistered together in the eighth house. Although Venus disposes of Mercury and the Sun (the co rulers of the subject) and indicates a strong attraction from the boy to the girl he is visiting, this conjunction will likely come into play through the course of this event. Saturn starts out in the twelfth house. Ordinarily a marker in a forming death pattern, this placement can serve as an omen of other aspects still not formed. And, finally, Neptune is in the fourth house. Right away, I say that Neptune represents the girl he was visiting and the fact that her identity has always been kept secret and she was never interviewed about the case. But it also shows us a secret relationship between Keith and the girl in question and I am not saying it had to be sex. You tell me what you think it was.

Roll the charts forward in 30 minute increments until you see something change. In these charts, it happens here:

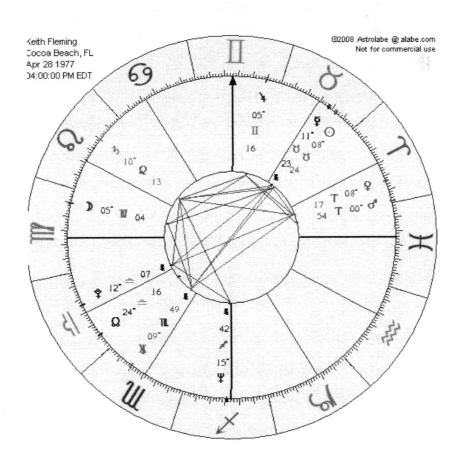

In this chart, you see the changes happening. Neptune has left the fourth for the third house. The first house ruler, Mercury, has left the ninth. Pluto has entered the first house and the Venus- Mars conjunction has entered the seventh house. The are BIG changes. They reported that Keith left the house with the girl on a bicycle and went out to the highway to walk and hitchhike. Here you see Neptune, the seventh house ruler (and marker for the girl) moving through the third house. Usually this would mean a car but it can be any vehicle and we know the girl was too young to drive. The reports have him on the bicycle with the girl. Although the charts are never that detailed, we can see that she has left the house in or on a vehicle and Keith has followed her. His current location has changed from inside to outside. How do we know that? The fourth house ruler, Jupiter, has left the tenth house for the ninth, showing us his new location is outdoors. The ninth house can be a highway. Jupiter in Gemini fits the descriptors as well, being that A1A, the highway he traveled on, runs the whole course of the state of Florida and is a major coastal highway system. Gemini fits perfectly as A1A is two laned on both sides, has many branches and exits and is heavily trafficked. The fact here that Mercury now rules both the tenth and the first houses brings it all together. It certainly looks like he was taken up to the highway on or in a vehicle (said to be a bike) and then traveled along that highway afterwards.

So the charts are showing us that Keith left that girl's house alive and well, got on a bike with her, went to the highway and started on his way home, as reported. He was going to walk part of the way and hitchhike for rides as well. I lived in that area during the 1970s and remember picking up hitchhikers all the time and once in awhile sticking out my thumb for a ride. It was commonplace and, for the most part, pretty safe. In time, there were abductions and murders involving hitchhikers (most famously the kidnappings and murders committed by Gerald Stano) and girls stopped doing it as much as they once had. Boys, however, never did think they had anything to fear.

So we know that Keith disappeared somewhere between leaving his friend's and getting on to A1A, heading home. Here is the next chart:

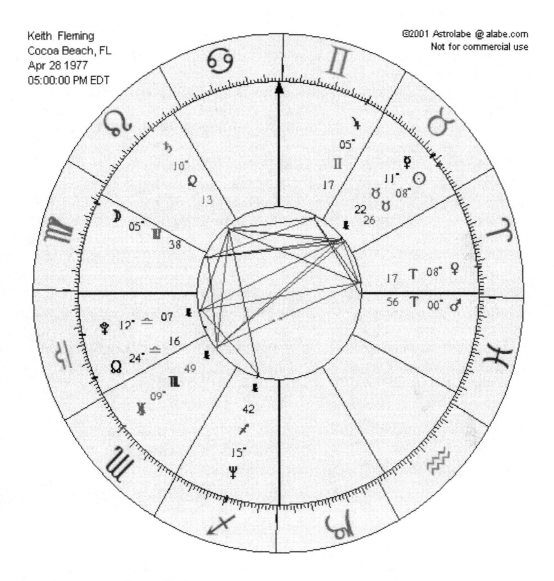

Keith Fleming
Cocoa Beach, FL
Apr 28 1977
05:00:00 PM EDT

I admit that what I do is run charts for every 30 minutes and when I see things changing, I may even run charts for every few minutes. I am always looking for the next big change that emphasis an important aspect or marker. At this moment, in this chart, the first house ruler has switched to Libra and Venus and Mars are hanging around the descendant. Scorpio is one degree on the third cusp with Pluto rising to the first. This shows us the car appearing and Venus, which marks the subject, is now with Mars, the seventh house ruler. A car has arrived and Keith has met his abductor. This chart is so important it can't be emphasized enough. STUDY IT. Always study intensely any chart that brings a change that is clearly a harbinger for things to come. Pluto in the first with Mars at the descendant should grab your attention. These aspects are only going to intensify as the cusps roll off the zero mark. This is the first inkling we get that the abductor is described by Mars. Mars is in the sixth house so right away I think he's military. We have several navy bases around the area, with one to the north of the place where he was abducted. Check the charts now for direction. He had been hitchhiking south. So has the direction turned? The neighborhood marker is always the third house. Here we see that Pluto is in the first house, which is dead east. This area is right along the east coast, heading north to south on A1A. So this supports the coastline as the current neighborhood. In the previous charts, his current location (at that time) was shown by the fourth house. The fourth house was ruled by Sagittarius with Jupiter in Gemini in the ninth. Sagittarius is east by south and he was hitchhiking south (he was in the northern portion of Cocoa Beach, heading home which was in the central part south of there). As well, A1A takes an even more easterly turn from there as it heads south and more into the older part of the city. In fact, all of the locational markers in this chart show him heading south. The fourth house ruler, Jupiter, is in Gemini (west by south) in the ninth house (southwest). The tenth house ruler, Mercury, is in Taurus (south by east) in the eighth house (west by south)... over and over again. He is heading south and possibly southeast. This direction does not appear to change after he is picked up by this stranger. Venus and Mars, the first and seventh house rulers, are in the sign Aries, which indicates east.

I can tell you, being familiar with the area, that the air force base is southeast of Cocoa Beach, which is southeast of where Keith started out. It is possible this person was stationed on the base and took Keith back there instead of taking him home.

Here is the next chart:

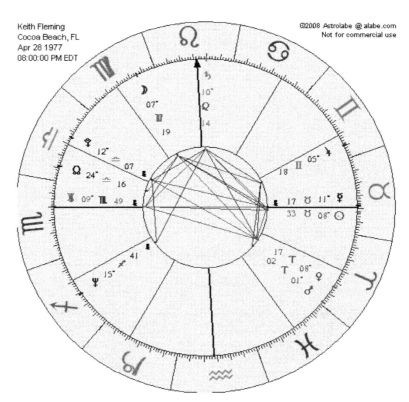

I chose to show you this chart next because it has so many descriptors. What do you see in this chart? What does it mean when Mars and Venus are together in the fifth house? What about Pluto in the eleventh? Notice that Pluto opposes the conjunction. Saturn is at the tenth house cusp. The Moon is in Virgo in the tenth. And Uranus, the fourth house ruler, has just crossed the ascendant into the twelfth house. Let me point out that the Moon is disposed of by Mercury, which is the traditional ruler for children, and Mercury is conjoined the seventh cusp. I want you to study the chart for awhile and then see if you can't discover what this chart is saying. Where is Keith Fleming? And what is happening to him?

I will give you my impressions after we look at one more case.

From the Charley Project :

Sharpless was last seen in Gladwyne, Pennsylvania at 4:45 a.m. on August 23, 2009. She left her home in West Brandywine Township, Pennsylvania to go out with a friend, Crystal Johns, that night. They originally went to the Ice Nightclub, then to a house party in the 1300 block of Bobarn Drive. At 3:00 a.m., Sharpless sent a text message to her twelve-year-old daughter. She later caused a disturbance at the party when she got angry with another guest and poured a bottle of champagne on the floor. She and Johns were asked to leave.

Both women had been drinking alcohol that evening, something Sharpless was not supposed to do because of the medication she was taking, and Sharpless had reportedly been awake for approximately 36 hours. She was angry and crying when she left the party with Johns. They had only driven a few blocks when they got into an argument because Johns didn't believe Sharpless was sober enough to drive. (Sharpless has a 2008 conviction for driving under the influence.) Sharpless stopped the car and demanded her friend get out, so Johns exited the vehicle and then Sharpless drove away. Johns initially assumed she would return. When she didn't come back, Johns had a relative come and pick her up instead. Sharpless has never been heard from again.

Sharpless was driving her black four-door 2002 Pontiac Grand Prix GT with tinted windows and the Pennsylvania license plate number DND7772 at the time of her disappearance. It has never been located. A photo of a similar vehicle is posted below this case summary. Someone ran the license plate number in Camden, New Jersey on September 8, two weeks after Sharpless disappeared. By the time Pennsylvania police were notified of this, several days had passed and they were unable to locate the car. Sharpless's cellular phone also remains missing and has been turned off since approximately 4:00 a.m. the day she disappeared.

According to Johns, Sharpless was low on gas, and it's possible she ran out of gas or turned in another direction to go get some. There were clusters of sightings of her reported in Lancaster, Pennsylvania; Philadelphia, Pennsylvania; and Camden, New Jersey after her disappearance. All of them took place in areas known for their prostitution and drug activity. None of the sightings have been confirmed. A private detective hired by Sharpless's family believes she may have be alive and may have gotten involved with drugs and the sex trade. She had had a drug problem in the past. Johns isn't considered a suspect in her disappearance, and neither is anyone else at the party Sharpless attended that night.

Here is the chart for when she was last seen:

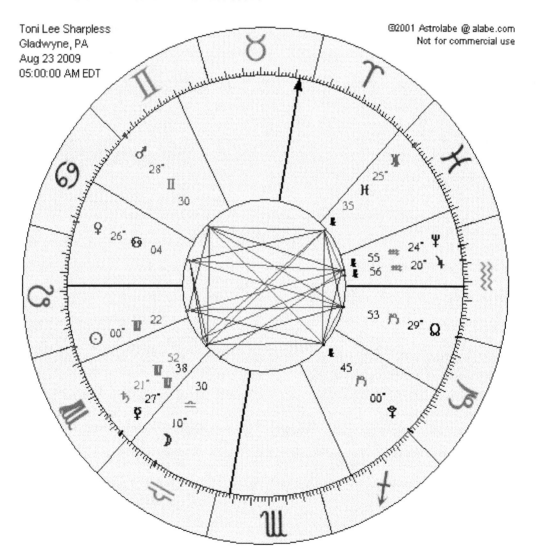

This chart is for the time her friend said she got out of Tonis' car. This would be the last time she was seen alive. Notice some of the aspects that fit the reported facts. The fourth house ruler, which shows her current or last location, is Pluto in the fifth house. She had been a party at a person's home. The Sun rules the first house and is also in the first house, showing Toni to be "full of herself" and doing whatever she wanted to. Moon in third in Libra verifies that she did get into a car and leave. Sun disposed of by Mercury in Virgo, which is conjoined with Saturn, indicates that she was criticized for something she said. Mars in eleventh in an out of sign opposition to Pluto shows that there was a bit of a confrontation or, at the least, an angry reprisal, at the party. Someone among her friends got angry at her. Mars in Gemini is also square to Mercury, with Mars ruling the fourth house, so she said something rude and was ousted from the party. All of this fits. The charts appear to support the facts so we will call the chart viable. But the most important thing here, if you were to be looking at this chart in the hopes of finding out what happened to Toni, would be what? What would you look at as a harbinger of the future?

One thing that stands out for me is the seventh house ruler, Uranus, in the eighth house. The seventh house is always the person we are "next to meet" or about to meet, as they say. The seventh house ruler in the eighth house ALWAYS depicts a criminal or sleazy type person who steals or lies or lives on the edge of society. Especially when it is in a sign like Pisces and in mutual reception with Neptune in the seventh. The seventh house ruler, by the way, is Uranus. Uranus is known for fringe personality types, people who don't play by the rules and also people that do surprising things. Notice that Neptune is conjoined to Jupiter, a marker for overindulgence if there ever was one. We know Toni was drunk that night but the person she was about to meet was most likely high on drugs.

At this point, the questions you might be asking would include where she met this person, why they came together at all, what happened after she met up with this person and where did they go? We know that Toni is in her car (Moon in the third) and traveling west (Libra on the cusp). Noting that the Moon is disposed of by Venus and also in mutual reception with Venus (in the sign Cancer in the twelfth house) so it would be Venus that would give us clues about Toni's plans. The disposition of a planet shows the purpose or aim in that planet's movements. It is a tough guess with this one, though, because of the circumstances. The twelfth house can indicate many things, from going about doing something in secret or trying to hide from other people to being captured and trapped and held captive or looking for drugs or alcohol to stay high or to go to sleep. Of course, it can also mean someone is simply trying to get to bed. What do you think it's in this case? Does the first house Sun placement rule out certain possiblities? Doesn't it seem that she is "in charge"? Would this make the captive or abducted scenario seem impossible? You decide.

Here is the next chart:

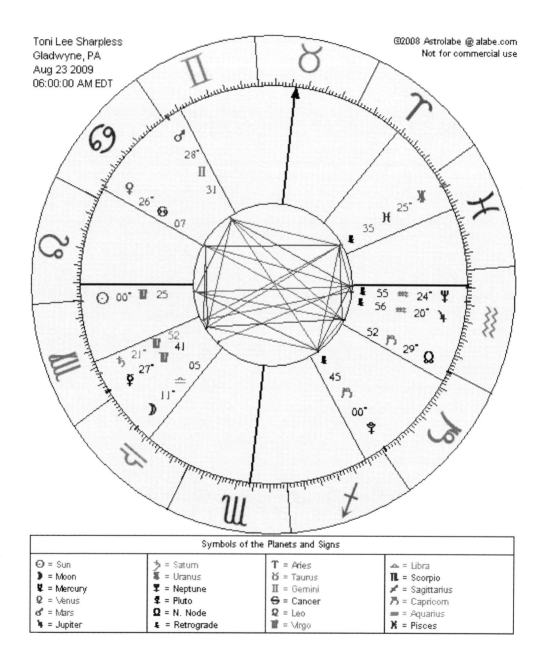

This chart is drawn for the next hour after Toni went missing. It should give us some insight into what was happening during this event. The Moon is now in the second house, disposed of by Venus in the eleventh. Venus also rules the tenth house. The seventh house ruler, Uranus, is still in the eighth. Neptune and Jupiter are in the sixth house of health. Pluto, the fourth house ruler, remains in the fifth. Doesn't this look like the subject wanted the party to continue (Venus in the eleventh with Pluto in the fifth) and was considering buying something that would help keep it going? Neptune and

Jupiter in the sixth show us that her health was already challenged by the overindulgence in drugs or alcohol but Sun in the first shows us someone still going strong and doing what she wanted to. The Sun is disposed of by Mercury, which is now in the second, along with the Moon. Doesn't this look like she's getting money for a transaction of some sort? With Neptune at the descendant and Uranus still ruling the seventh from the eighth, it looks to me like she hooked up with a drug dealer (a criminal) to obtain drugs. This doesn't look like a trip to the 7-11 for beer. Or does it? What does it seem to be from your perspective? That is your job when you do this work, to try to figure out what the subject is doing. So study this chart and come to your own conclusions. I just gave you my first impressions.

More impressions coming to me is that Toni was hiding a sadness or heartbreak. I see this by the conjunction of Mercury with Saturn, which is a critical aspect pointing to depression, self reprisal or unncessary criticism of others. This conjunction is closely opposed to Uranus in the eighth. Uranus rules the seventh so this may be a "go to" person for her when she is feeling down. Reports have it that she had a drug problem in the past. If she had been depressed over something and this is why she was drinking to begin with, perhaps she escalated to drugs after the party. It's possible. Another aspect that requires attention is the mutual reception between the Moon and Venus with Venus closely trine to the seventh house ruler. This looks like a sexual attraction to me, or at the very least, a sexual contact. Since the Moon is in the second house, perhaps she planned to use sex as payment for the drugs? Could it be that her friends are right? She ended up in the sex industry? You have to study these charts to see if that fits the overall picture.

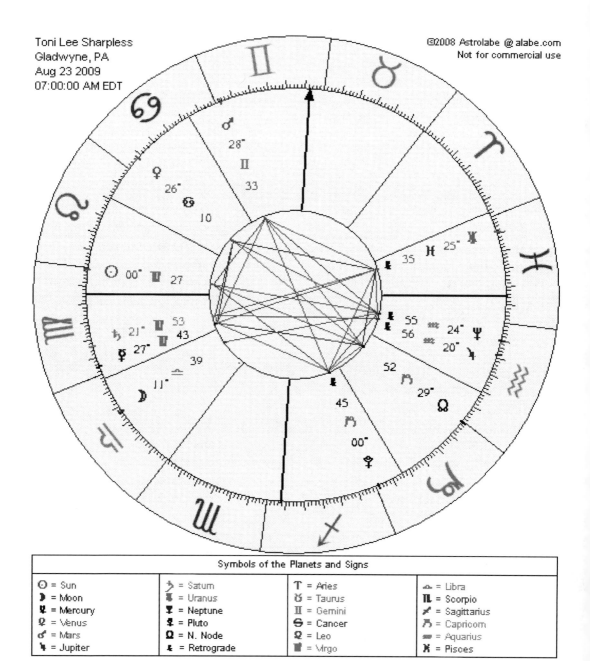

Toni Lee Sharpless
Gladwyne, PA
Aug 23 2009
07:00:00 AM EDT

©2008 Astrolabe @ alabe.com
Not for commercial use

Symbols of the Planets and Signs			
☉ = Sun	♄ = Saturn	♈ = Aries	♎ = Libra
☽ = Moon	♅ = Uranus	♉ = Taurus	♏ = Scorpio
☿ = Mercury	♆ = Neptune	♊ = Gemini	♐ = Sagittarius
♀ = Venus	♇ = Pluto	♋ = Cancer	♑ = Capricorn
♂ = Mars	☊ = N. Node	♌ = Leo	♒ = Aquarius
♃ = Jupiter	℞ = Retrograde	♍ = Virgo	♓ = Pisces

This is two hours after Toni was last seen and there are no markers for abduction. There is no death pattern. When the Sun slips into the twelfth, it is after Virgo takes over the ascendant, which makes Mercury her marker. Mercury is in the first house now, just as the Sun was when Leo was on the first. This is what I call consistant. It is telling you, again, that Toni is doing what she wants to and is traveling under her own steam. There are some key changes in the patterns, as well, that start to tell us the next chapter in this story. Neptune now rules the seventh and it is in the sixth house along with Jupiter, which rules the fourth. I am not going to tell you what I think at this point. I want you to study these charts and come up with your own analysis. I have given you my first impressions and I want you to take it from here. But I will point out the aspects and placements that matter. Neptune conjoined Jupiter in the sixth house is a big one. Mars has gone angular in the tenth while both Saturn and Mercury have joined each other in the first house. Moon is still in the second, in the same configuration with Venus. So now, it's up to you.

In the Keith Fleming case, I am hoping you gave the last chart some thought. I will tell you that my first impression is that the two of them have gone to the abductors home and a sexual assault occurred there. Now you take it from there.

Made in the USA
Middletown, DE
06 April 2015